JUDSON PRESS
PUBLISHERS SINCE 1824

Tending to Eden

Environmental Stewardship for God's People

SCOTT C. SABIN

Kathy Ide, editor

Foreword by Brian McLaren

JUDSON PRESS
PUBLISHERS SINCE 1824
VALLEY FORGE, PA

www.PlantWithPurpose.org

Mission: Plant With Purpose, a Christian non-profit organization, reverses deforestation and poverty in the world, by transforming the lives of the rural poor. We plant, we teach, we create enterprise, and we share the gospel.

Library of Congress Cataloging-in-Publication Data
Sabin, Scott C.
    Tending to Eden : environmental stewardship for God's people / Scott C. Sabin; Kathy Ide, editor; foreword by Brian McLaren. — 1st ed.
        p. cm.
    ISBN 978-0-8170-1572-5 (pbk. : alk. paper) 1. Environmentalism—Religious aspects—Christianity. 2. Human ecology—Religious aspects—Christianity. 3. Christian life. I. Ide, Kathy. II. Title.

BT695.5.S23   2010
261.8'8—dc22

                                                            2009046832

Contents

Foreword

Thank you. Thank you for picking up this book and for reading it and for letting it influence you. Thanks for opening your mind to some new ideas, and then letting those new ideas influence the way you live, and then letting your changing way of life influence others in your circle of family and friends. Thank you.

Thank you for doing something good for yourself because your life will be more full and wise having learned from Scott Sabin in these pages. In return for the time you invest in this book, you will gain freedom from the ignorance and misinformation that cloud the thinking and inhibit the constructive action of so many people, including many sincere Christians. After reading this very readable book with its powerful storytelling and its accessible survey of best practices in creation care, for the rest of your life you will see a bigger picture than you've ever seen before when it comes to matters of human poverty, health, prosperity, and security.

Thanks for enriching your spiritual development, because when we understand ourselves as God's creatures woven into the fabric of God's world, we take our proper place in the big scheme of things, which brings blessing to us and to all whose lives we touch.

Thank you for doing something good for the world. The world needs us—you and me and millions more of us—to have a change in mind and heart about our relationship to the beautiful planet to which we have been given by God as caretakers, and which has been given to us for enjoyment and in stewardship. By reading this book, you will render yourself more vulnerable to that kind of change in mind and heart.

Thanks on behalf of a little girl walking a dusty road in Haiti, because by learning about her connection to the land, you can help her find a better future.

Thanks on behalf of a woman and her children in southern Mexico whose husband had to head north seeking work because their farmlands no longer produce. By reading this book, you can become part of the solution to the far-reaching economic and ecological problems that have divided this dad from his wife and kids, plunging them all into insecurity.

Thanks on behalf of thousands of children who, because of the combined efforts of readers of this book, will not have to grow up in miserable slums ringing major cities around our world. By reading these chapters, we will learn how to make it possible for these kids to be raised in villages where caring people know their names and recognize their laughter, connected to the land and its fresh air and clean water, instead of being trapped in crime-ridden slums amidst mountains of trash, fetid with human excrement and disease.

And thanks on behalf of God's creatures who have no voices or language to speak up for themselves . . . for songbirds and monkeys, for turtles and butterflies, for wildflowers and coral. As you read this book, you'll understand that you are their advocate and that they depend on you to be sure they aren't plowed under or burned up or squeezed out by human beings who don't know what you know or feel what you feel because of reading this book. When they sing or fly or swim or bloom or grow and reproduce, that will be their way of thanking you.

Reading a book doesn't change the world any more than writing one does. But when writers and readers are informed and inspired, they can take action together, and when that happens, change isn't just possible; it's inevitable.

I've walked the same kinds of streets Scott writes about in this book. I've observed the little girls and boys sorting through trash. I've smelled the sewage, seen the flies, and swatted the mosquitoes. I've seen the erosion ditches measured in feet and yards, not inches, grabbed handfuls of the depleted and sun-baked soil, witnessed the refugees lining the streets in search of a few dollars' worth of hope . . . on their road to somewhere, anywhere more green. I've seen treeless hills, the charcoal pits, the bush meat hanging in the markets, the distended bellies, the girls walking for miles for water or firewood . . . all signs that the sacred covenant of balance between people and the land has been broken.

And I've met many of the people who work with Scott in teaching people how to restore the covenant. I've heard their stories of helping people find the right trees and crops and farming practices so that their lives are filled with much less desperation and much more shalom. I've felt their passion for wisely using every dollar donated to micro-enterprise, micro-finance, and sustainable farming. I've seen their eyes light up when they find someone who is beginning to "get it" when it comes to the spirituality of ecology and stewardship of the land, themes about which the Bible has so much to teach.

That's why I care so much about the message of this book, and that's why I'm so glad you're going to read it. That's why I'm so hopeful that, as you read, you might join the Plant with Purpose movement, seeking to restore our world so that it looks a lot more like Eden and feels a lot less like hell. That's why, from the bottom of my heart, I say once more, *thank you.*

Brian McLaren
Laurel, Maryland

Acknowledgments

I would like to thank the many people who made this book possible—it is far more of a team effort than I ever expected. Sarah Ferry and Aly Lewis originally conceived and pushed the idea when I was reluctant to get started. Rebecca Buckham did much of the work on the Bible study, which was the seed from which the rest of the book grew. Bob Morikawa and Deann Alford gave significant time and wisdom, reading over earlier versions and saving me from considerable embarrassment. Corbyn Small, Nick Wiik, Nathan Lack, Warren Howe, Jimmy Lee, Gabe Lupin, and Mikaela Akesson helped with research, fact checking, and myriad other tasks. I also want to thank those who contributed sidebars and case studies. I am deeply honored. Thanks to my editor, Kathy Ide, for all her work and encouragement, and to Rebecca Irwin-Diehl and the team at Judson Press for giving me this opportunity. The staff of Plant With Purpose who kept things running so smoothly during the many days I was away writing deserve a great deal of gratitude, as do our board of directors. I am also deeply indebted to all the Floresta field staff who have taught me so much and done so much to transform the world. It is truly a privilege to be on a team with heroes. Finally, thank you to Nancy, my wife, who is always my first and final editor. She and my children, Amanda and Danny, have been extremely patient and longsuffering over the past months. Thank you.

Introduction

As rain swept across the canyon toward the jagged ridge where Eldon Garcia and I stood, I felt a long way from home. We were lost somewhere in the hills of southern Haiti—and our truck was nearly out of gas.

We had no choice but to return to Port-au-Prince. But as I looked at the nameless mountains surrounding us and the muddy ruts departing in several directions, I wondered: Where is Port-au-Prince?

I was the new acting director of Floresta USA, (now Plant With Purpose, although many of our field partners retain the Floresta name) a small Christian relief and development agency working in partnership with its Dominican counterpart, which Eldon directed. Eldon and I were exploring a possible collaboration with an Episcopal priest working in the mountains south of Port-au-Prince. It was early 1995, a few months after the U.S. invasion. Although I was interested in visiting Haiti, I wasn't all that excited about working there. Among its many disparaging titles, Haiti is known as the graveyard of good intentions.

However, Floresta Dominican Republic has an office in Santo Domingo, just across the island, and Eldon thought it would be simple enough to drive to Port-au-Prince. Once there, we would meet the woman facilitating the connection and follow her party to the mountains where Pere Wilfrid Albert, the priest, lived.

I had been working for Plant With Purpose for almost two years, drawn there by my interest in helping the poor and the fact that the organization was located in my hometown. I didn't have any particular interest in reforestation or the environment; in fact, I saw those things as a bit of a distraction. When people I met said, "Oh, that's the organization that plants the trees," I became annoyed, wanting to reply, "No, we are the organization that feeds the poor."

Of course, I had heard the story of how Plant With Purpose was created to address deforestation, a root cause of poverty. I could even repeat it and sound convincing. But I wasn't sure I fully believed it. Still, this job was temporary. I was only here to get some experience before applying for a job with a more established agency.

After Eldon and I crossed the border into Haiti, it felt like we were driving on the moon. The landscape was empty, stark, and utterly foreign. Haiti's largest lake, Étang Saumâtre, glistened a brilliant blue on our right. On the left, wasted brown mountains rose ominously. Occasionally we passed small quarries of white rock, full of workers wielding picks.

Since red tape at the border had made us nearly a day late, we had to change our plans. Rather than meeting our contacts in Port-au-Prince and accompanying them into the mountains south of Leogane, we would have to make our way into the mountains on our own. We were told to ask for directions from the staff of the Episcopal hospital in Leogane.

As we approached Port-au-Prince, the ramshackle homes became closer together, road conditions got worse, and traffic slowed. We soon found ourselves in a stream of brightly painted pickup trucks and buses packed with people. These buses, known as "tap taps," are typical public transport in Haiti.

Suddenly, Port-au-Prince loomed all around us. It looked as if the tide had come in over the cinderblock-and-iron architecture and stranded garbage and rubble on every horizontal surface. Human beings spilled out onto the broken streets, in every sort of dress imaginable. A naked man walked past a gentleman in a pin-striped suit, who was picking his way through the debris. People filled each alley and turned every sidewalk into an impromptu market. Rotting fruit and raw sewage odors combined with the smell of frying meat and exhaust. UN convoys of white SUVs and armored personnel carriers passed frequently.

At the port we turned south to follow the water. We got lost at one point and stopped to ask directions at a market situated on top of a heap of mango peels. The directions were incomprehensible, but we continued on National One, heading south, then west through the seemingly endless traffic jam of Carrefour.

Waiting for the traffic to move, we witnessed hundreds of mini-dramas. A truck, open in the back, sat in front of us, packed with market women sitting on bags of charcoal and rice. To the right, a small boy maneuvered a marionette deftly over the broken sidewalk. Further on, a broken pipe spilled into the gutter, providing an opportunity for women to do their laundry, while children crowded around, filling pails and jugs to take home.

Traffic ground to a halt again. Dozens of tap taps sat in the sweltering heat, jammed with solemn, sweating faces, while a pedestrian tide of incredible variety passed by them.

Finally, the congestion of the city thinned. We passed palm-thatched restaurants and small, ruined resorts. In the brilliant bay, wooden fishing boats created a picturesque backdrop. The tranquility and timelessness of the scene seemed incongruous with the nightmare of the previous months. I wondered how many of these fishermen had been tempted to participate in the recent exodus when, according to the news, anything that would float was pressed into service to escape the island.

The road became increasingly rutted. For several miles we moved at a painful crawl, weaving around and bouncing over huge potholes. Oncoming traffic frequently passed on the right as each driver sought a passable piece of road.

Without too much difficulty we found the hospital in Leogane, where we were told that Pere Albert would be easy to find. "Follow the highway south, toward Jacmel, until you come to your first right." We were to keep going until we saw a white church. Then we would be in Grand Colline.

As we followed the road climbing high above the valley, every slope was cultivated with struggling cornfields. Though we were far from any recognizable town, there was still a constant parade of pedestrians down either side of the road: old women leading donkeys, men carrying machetes, and groups of children in ragged yellow uniforms with big, reproachful eyes. But we never saw anything that resembled "our first right."

When we were almost to the beach, we found a dirt track leading into the mountains. It didn't feel right, but it lay vaguely in the direction we wanted to go, so we rumbled off into the hills. People along the way watched silently as we drove by.

We tried to ask for directions. But since we didn't speak Creole, we were forced to simply repeat, "Pere Albert? Grand Colline?" in hopes that someone would point.

As we drove higher into the mountains, I noticed stone tombs, built to look like tiny houses or cathedrals, in small clusters on the hilltops. Fog rolled in, reducing our visibility to a few hundred yards. The bleating of goats sounded almost like the wailing of lost souls.

We came to a familiar-looking crossroads. We had been there before . . . but on the other road.

We soon met a girl of maybe fourteen, whose face lit up when we said, "Pere Albert?" She jumped into the back of the truck and said with assurance, "We go!" But in a few minutes she seemed to lose confidence.

After a couple of hours, Eldon noticed the gas gauge nearing empty. "We need to get back to Port-au-Prince," he said. "But which way?" We made a U-turn.

Eldon turned to me. "Scott, what are we going to do about this girl?"

No suitable answer came to mind. "I don't know," I said feebly. "Maybe we should tell her to get out." She would be better off than we were, I rationalized.

The road appeared to end at a cliff just past a small market. As we got out of the car to investigate, rain began to fall. The market crowd eyed us warily.

When we returned to the car, Eldon couldn't find the key. For a few minutes we stood in the pouring rain. The crowd edged nearer. I wondered what kind of hospitality could be expected from these villagers if we ran out of gas. And I wondered how I'd ended up lost in these mountains so far from home.

Eventually Eldon and I decided to pray. We knew God had brought us this far for a reason.

Almost immediately after we said, "Amen," Eldon found the key. It was stuck in the driver's side door.

We headed in the direction we thought Port-au-Prince should be, still wondering what was the right thing to do with the girl. After we forded a small stream and started up the hill on the other side, several more children jumped in the back of the truck. Eldon didn't stop.

About a mile later, our young friend leaned into the cab and in plain, unaccented English said, "Stop! Stop!" She and the rest of the children jumped from the truck and ran to meet their friends. Behind a small grove of trees stood a white church. As I stepped out of the truck, a tall Haitian man came from the house nearby and wrapped me in a bear hug. We had found Pere Albert!

The three of us sat around a table and talked long into the night, our faces illuminated by a propane lantern. Pere Albert described the local struggle for survival. I learned he had almost single-handedly founded thirty schools in the parish and was now responsible for the education of more than eleven thousand children. The next morning we visited some nearby fields, where farmers eked out a living from the rocky mountainsides.

I had no intention of devoting my life to environmental issues. Yet somewhere on that trip, it dawned on me that they were foundational. The suffering masses in Port-au-Prince had come there because they felt they had more opportunity in that squalor than in the countryside.

The quaint, bucolic scenes of rural life hid a horror just beneath the surface. Every bit of land was used up, depleted, and divided, yet still was being used as farmland. Trucks rumbled past, hauling charcoal down from the mountains, creating more desert. In his book *The Immaculate Invasion*, Bob Shacochis described these same mountains:

[It was] the saddest mountain range on the planet, the first mountains I had ever seen that made me want to vomit, a line of ravaged peaks like a ward of cancer patients, a hardwood tropical forest from horizon to horizon reduced to little more than rain-crumbled rock.[1]

Sadly, this is an apt description. Yet it makes me feel a bit defensive. Today, I know those mountains, and I know the people who live in them. I've developed a deep love and a great deal of respect for these people. I know their dreams, their courage, and the incredible persistence with which they work to take care of their families. I know the lack of opportunity that has made the destruction of this land inevitable. I also believe God knows those mountains and their people. He loves them and has a plan to redeem them and bless them.

As I observed these mountains, I realized how fundamental the work of reforestation and restoration is to the needs of the poor. And somehow I knew God was calling me to this ministry.

At the time I didn't realize how strongly the Bible encourages us to be stewards of God's creation. I didn't understand that caring for the environment is good and necessary because it shows respect and love for the Creator. I just knew people needed trees.

Five Relationships

I have traveled a long way, both figuratively and literally, since that afternoon on the ridge in Haiti—and I have learned a great deal.

First, I have learned that helping the poor in a significant way is considerably more difficult than I originally thought. I naïvely believed helping the poor would be fairly simple. I think most people underestimate the challenges involved.

Poverty stems from much more than a lack of resources. It can't be fixed just by giving more money or more stuff. In truth, poverty is a result of broken relationships as much as anything else. Anyone who has ever been part of a family knows fixing broken relationships is hard work, even if everyone is committed to the process.

When Plant With Purpose began, we looked to poverty's environmental roots, and we found this, too, was the result of a broken relationship: the relationship between human beings and the earth. As Plant With Purpose has grown, we have increasingly focused on four relationships that are key to any program hoping to bring lasting change. Jesus addressed two of these when a teacher of the law asked which commandment was most important. "The most important one," answered Jesus, "is this: . . . 'Love the Lord your God with all your heart and with all your soul and with all your mind and with all your strength.' The second is this: 'Love your neighbor as yourself.' There is no commandment greater than these" (Mark 12:29-31).

Our relationship with God is most important, and the second key relationship is with our neighbors. Jesus tells us we are to love him by caring for others. When Jesus was asked what that looked like, he responded with the parable of the Good Samaritan. Isaiah 58 and 1 John 4:20 give us further instruction on how to honor God in our relationships with other people.

Healing relationships is an important part of Plant With Purpose's discipleship programs. This emphasis is woven through our community organizing and the economic relationships we help to build. Our work is an expression of our love for God and neighbor.

There are two other relationships that are also important: our relationship with ourselves and our relationship with creation.

If we do not have an accurate view of who we are in God's universe, we will have a hard time loving anyone else. Many of us have an inflated sense of our importance and talents, which leads to pride, ignorance, and arrogance. On the other hand, others of us—especially those who are poor—tend to discount our importance and giftedness, which leads to helplessness and disempowerment. Both groups need to develop a more accurate understanding of who they are in relationship to God.

If we do not understand the tendency to distort our self-worth, especially as relationships are formed across cultures and economic classes, we can easily reinforce these distortions. Over and over I have witnessed well-meaning visitors from the United States strengthen their own self-image as saviors as they inadvertently add to the sense of helplessness among the poor. The church is becoming more involved in overseas ministry due to easier communication and travel. Plant With Purpose has much to share about what works and what doesn't work in serving the poor.

The relationship between humans and creation is a topic that is gaining interest as the limits of our planet and the need for a coherent response from the church become apparent. That relationship is often taken for granted, but it is a sacred one, carrying with it important responsibilities.

To heal humanity's relationship with creation, Plant With Purpose encourages reforestation and sustainable agriculture. Providing economic opportunities by encouraging local enterprise creation addresses the relationships between people, as it levels the playing field for the disadvantaged and helps families stay together. Discipleship focuses on our relationship with God. By helping others follow Jesus and obey his commandments, thus fulfilling the Great Commission, we help to create a foundation upon which future development can be built.

Once we see the impact of environmental issues in the lives of the poor overseas, we will see more clearly the impact of these issues here at home. We will find ways to better honor God and offer justice to our neighbors, the poor, and creation.

There is a fifth relationship: the relationship between the creation and God, the Creator. God has not forgotten his love for the world and covenant with creation. We are reminded of this forcefully in Job 38, and more gently in Psalm 104. These passages reflect God's joy over creation and creation's enjoyment of God.

God created the universe, considers it good, enjoys it, and has asked us to take care of our corner of it for him. It is a responsibility we should take seriously.

CHAPTER I

Discovering God's Heart for the World

In many ways my journey toward becoming an environmentalist began when I spent a summer in a Spanish immersion program in Guatemala. I was hoping to be a diplomat, and this program would fulfill the language requirement for a master's degree in international relations.

As a typical evangelical from the U.S. suburbs, I had grown up in the church and accepted Jesus at summer camp. My faith was personal but not particularly relevant to the problems of the world.

Guatemala gave a face to the problem of poverty. I was charmed by the country's colorful culture and its gentle people. My walk to class took me along cobblestone streets beneath a magnificent volcano. But the injustice and poverty were impossible to ignore. The long civil war that had wracked the nation, particularly the highlands, was winding down. Parts of the country were still not safe. Memories of massacres and death squads were fresh in people's minds.

Although I had seen poverty before, I'd never spent this much time up close to it. In Southern California we do a remarkable job of cordoning ourselves off from those who are less fortunate. We live in neighborhoods with people of similar socioeconomic status; we go to church with people just like us; and we commute on freeways full of vehicles, not people. Other than the panhandler at the intersection, who often looks like he could work if he wanted to, we can go for weeks without seeing a person noticeably poorer than ourselves. It's easy for many of us to forget there are people in our own backyard who are genuinely hungry. In Guatemala, as in most of the world, there is no convenient separation that allows the guilt-free enjoyment of privilege.

On weekdays I attended classes. On weekends God introduced me to missionaries, aid workers, local pastors, and ordinary Christians who were beacons of light in the darkness. I tend to be skeptical of overly spiritual interpretations of events, yet I can only see that time as miraculous.

One weekend, I visited a dump in Guatemala City. Acrid smoke curled into the sky behind the block wall surrounding it. Mountains of garbage smoldered beneath wheeling vultures. Amid heaps of rotting food, cardboard, and burning plastic, rag-clad little boys and girls sorted through the piles. I was stunned to learn that they and their families lived in this dump, fighting over the privilege of picking through the scraps.

When Jesus described the place of damnation, he called it *Gehenna*—the name of the garbage dump outside of Jerusalem. The image of hell as a refuse pile took on new meaning for me. This place was as close to hell on earth as I could imagine.

I then visited a school founded by a young American woman who recognized these children as her neighbors. Kari Engen and her Guatemalan colleagues had committed their lives to these children. Though she was a couple of years younger than me, she had already given five years to this place. In her early twenties she had actually lived with the families in the dump.

Two weeks later I met a Guatemalan pastor, Salomón Hernández, from the highlands of El Quiché, where the civil war had been most brutal. He told me of having guerrillas on one side of his house and the army on the other, while he and his wife offered tortillas and prayed with the combatants.

I accepted his invitation to travel to El Quiché to see his work firsthand. After spending half a day on a bus, I wandered near the market in Coban, looking for the next bus. An open truck with a dozen locals in back pulled alongside me. The driver said, "Get in." I joined people, chickens, and produce as we banged over a dirt road into the hills. The young woman upwind of me began to vomit. When the rain came, we pulled a tarp over us. A couple of miles out of town, the truck broke down. At dusk, I finally arrived on Salomón Hernández's doorstep.

The next morning he took me to meet the members of his extended church, people devastated by violence and oppression. What could have been grim was made beautiful by his buoyant spirit. We rattled over the dirt roads in his rusty pickup, listening to classical music and laughing. His compassion was as abundant as his joy.

We drove from farm to farm, visiting widows and children in their tiny ramshackle homes, listening to stories of rape and murder. Yet there was a sense of healing; they had found it in their hearts to forgive. Salomón's joyous outlook in the face of so much pain and brutality was evidence of a depth of faith new to me.

The day I was to leave, as we looked out over corn-laden hills, he said, "Visitors come to Guatemala and see the beautiful mountains full of quaint villages. They think this is a pretty place and life is good. But I want you to remember the people you've met and their struggle."

I knew I would never forget them, nor would I forget Salomón or others whom I had met who were so courageously sharing the love of Jesus.

The woman working with Wycliffe who had lost her husband to malaria years earlier in Papua New Guinea, but continued in her calling despite her loneliness.

The Canadian couple building latrines to improve sanitation in remote villages.

The missionary who kept preaching the gospel in spite of death threats.

The injustice and poverty were frightening and heavy. But in the grimmest situations, God was there, working through someone to bring redemption. In those dark places the light was most obvious, most alive. Furthermore, the tangible way God showed me what he wanted me to see was thrilling and addicting. God was guiding my every step, sometimes so clearly that others around me noticed. I realized following Jesus could be far more exciting than I'd ever imagined.

Like most people, I had heard about Mother Teresa but thought of her as unique. I began to see there was a whole army of lesser-known Mother Teresas working with incredible courage to share the light of Christ's love. I wanted to be around those kinds of people.

After returning home I heard Tony Campolo preach on power and sacrificial love. He concluded with a call to action, challenging his listeners to work with the poor. Rising to a crescendo, he asked why we would want to settle for a job in corporate America when we could be heroes.

I wanted to be a hero! Or at least I wanted to be part of a team that had heroes on it.

Faithful to the Vision

Most of us long to be part of something bigger than ourselves. Our consumer-oriented culture has done a miserable job of giving us any sense of purpose. Yet mainstream Christianity has often failed to provide an alternative.

Fresh off my summer in Guatemala, and on the heels of the Los Angeles riots, I asked a pastor what he saw as the biggest challenge facing the church. I yearned to hear how Christians might confront racism and injustice. Instead, he responded with concern over the church's upcoming fundraising campaign to raise money for its new office building.

To be fair, the pastor had misinterpreted the question. But my sense of betrayal was compounded when I saw the campaign, crafted around the idea that "people without a vision perish." Expensive banners called the congregation to be "Faithful to the Vision." It was effective fundraising, but the scale of the vision made a mockery of the kingdom of God.

The body of Christ is the only hope for a hurting and unjust world. God help us when our biggest visions are limited to building campaigns.

Justice as an Act of Worship

Worship is meant to be the work of the whole created order. The world was fashioned in love, to embody and proclaim the worthiness and glory of our Creator in all relationships: toward God, our neighbors, ourselves, and the earth.

The song of creation is meant to magnify the beauty, order, imagination, and purposes of our God. This requires appropriate use of the power God has placed in creation—and within human beings in particular. The stewardship of the earth, or creation care, affirms this. When our relationships with God, our neighbors, and the earth are honored by this sort of faithful stewardship, creation sings and God is joyfully and truly worshiped.

However, this is often not how the story goes. Injustices of all kinds point to distortions of power that lead in turn to abuses of creation, ourselves, our neighbors, and God. That causes worship to fail and creation's song to falter. In order for worship to be renewed, we must realign power for life-giving, creation-honoring purposes so our lives will again attend to what matters to God, so our relationships will be renewed, and so every part of creation can freely sing the glory God is due.

Mark Labberton is associate professor of the Lloyd John Ogilvie Chair of Preaching and director of the Lloyd John Ogilvie Institute for Preaching at Fuller Theological Seminary.

The message of the church has often been that what we do in this life doesn't really matter as long as we avoid certain sins such as drinking, swearing, and fornicating. God has already won the battle, and we just have to stay out of trouble until Jesus returns to take us away.

But the Christian life isn't only about what *not* to do. We have a role in bringing the justice, hope, and peace of Christ to the world. God has given us an active role in his grand story of the redemption of the universe. How many people outside the church would be drawn in if they saw us bringing justice, hope and peace?

I am heartened by the renewed interest in social justice I see within the church, especially among youth. Today I meet twenty-three-year-old college students at the same point in their vocational development I reached at age thirty-two. Social justice is now fashionable. I hope it is more than merely a fad.

Call to Justice

Justice has always been one of the primary callings of God's people. Jesus began his ministry reading from Isaiah 61:

> The Spirit of the Lord is on me, because he has anointed me to preach good news to the poor. He has sent me to proclaim freedom for the prisoners and recovery of sight for the blind, to set the oppressed free. (Luke 4:18)

As we proclaim the good news of God's kingdom, we are to live as if the kingdom is at hand.

We see a similar theme in Isaiah 58, where God admonishes Israel for over-spiritualizing worship without changing their behavior. They genuinely believed they were right before God, doing what he wanted in their worship and seeking a closer relationship with him. In verses 2-3, God says, "Day after day they seek me out; they seem eager to know my ways, as if they were a nation that does what is right. . . . 'Why have we fasted,' they say, 'and you have not seen it?'"

They missed the point. Their spiritual disciplines had no effect on their behavior. God reminds them:

> On the day of your fasting, you do as you please. . . .
> You cannot fast as you do today
> and expect your voice to be heard on high.
> Is this the kind of fast I have chosen,
> only a day for people to humble themselves? . . .
> Is that what you call a fast,
> a day acceptable to the LORD?
>
> —Isaiah 58:4-5

God's expectations, then and now, have little to do with personal piety and everything to do with how we treat others. God's fast is about something other than abstaining from food.

> Is not this the kind of fasting I have chosen:
> to loose the chains of injustice
> to set the oppressed free . . .
> Is it not to share your food with the hungry
> and to provide the poor wanderer with shelter—
> when you see the naked, to clothe them?
>
> —Isaiah 58:6-7

God's Word is clear on what we must do for our light to shine in the darkness. The good news must be shared by demonstration as well as proclamation. Isaiah 58:10 sums it up: "If you spend yourselves in behalf of the hungry and satisfy the needs of the oppressed, then your light will rise in the darkness, and your night will become like the noonday."

I love the image of spending ourselves. The church people I met in Guatemala were spending themselves on behalf of the hungry. That was what first drew me to them. It was a grand vision of God's kingdom, a purpose worth pursuing.

I wonder what would happen if we in the American church became known for spending ourselves on behalf of the hungry. I'm not talking about the efforts of just a few aid organizations that disguise their Christianity to better appeal to secular donors, but the entire U.S. church. How would our reputation in the world change? Could we become a beacon of hope to a hurting world?

Love God, Love Your Neighbor

When Jesus was asked what the most important commandments were, he summarized the law with two: Love the Lord your God with all your heart, soul, strength, and mind, and love your neighbor as yourself. Sadly, our neighbors are often invisible to us.

In our well-to-do enclaves, it's easy to forget about the needy. Nearly half the world survives on less than $2.50 a day.[1] An estimated 27 million people live as slaves.[2] Desperation leads many people to risk their lives for the privilege of working on the margins of our society, hoping to give their children a better opportunity.

The missions movement has been instrumental in making North American Christians more aware of the need in our world. Short-term trips can help us develop compassion for our neighbors. However, they should be seen primarily as a learning experience rather than our ultimate response.

Once we recognize our neighbor, the next step is acting. Being a Good Samaritan requires taking personal responsibility for what we see. In Matthew 25, Jesus equates our treatment of the marginalized with how we treat him. But most people don't even cross the road when they observe a need.

Finding Balance

I came home from Guatemala excited to share my discoveries. But the lack of interest shown by many other Christians surprised me. Perhaps my inability to communicate was partially to blame. However, the call to justice has always been problematic. The Israelites to whom Isaiah spoke missed it. At the time of Christ, the most religiously observant missed it. The early church missed it. We too are prone to miss it.

There is a pitfall on the opposite extreme as well: forsaking the proclamation of the gospel even as we get the demonstration of it right. The "social gospel" movement of a century ago emphasized justice at the expense of evangelism. In reaction, many evangelicals shrank from mercy ministries and are only now beginning to recover from that rejection.

As more people in the church begin to realize the gospel applies to this life as much as the next, we are in danger of forgetting its eternal implications. Demonstration and proclamation must be as one, or we rob Christ's message of its vitality. Some have called these the two hands of the gospel, but hands often work independently of each another. Gustavo Crocker, former director of Nazarene

Compassionate Ministries, compared them more accurately to two wings that must work together in order to be effective.

Christian parents don't agonize over whether it is more important to feed and clothe their children or to share Christ with them. We would never question putting immense energy into the physical well-being of our children, even if we believed that their eternal souls were of the greatest importance. By the same token, few Christian parents would bring up their children without teaching them about Jesus. If we did, we wouldn't be fully demonstrating love for them. It seems natural that we look after both the physical and spiritual needs of our children. Why should it be so difficult to achieve the same balance in loving our neighbors?

To really love our neighbors, we must address both their spiritual and physical needs. We need to invest ourselves in their lives, just as Christ invested himself in the lives of his disciples.

Opportunities to be Good Samaritans surround us, and the possibilities for acting on our compassion have never been greater. If we do, there is no telling where the journey will lead. My own Christian journey has led to a passion for environmental stewardship, or creation care, as it has become known. Where might God be leading you?

CHAPTER 2

A Vicious Cycle

Looking for a way to spend myself for the hungry, I began volunteering for Plant With Purpose, simply because it was the Christian anti-poverty organization closest to my home. Mine was a humble beginning: stuffing response cards into envelopes and calling donors.

I wasn't totally comfortable with the environmental aspect of the work. My father's reaction didn't help. "Planting trees for Jesus?" he said. "That's as marginal as you can get." I wasn't entirely sure he was wrong. In fact, I hoped to move as soon as I could to another organization that was doing more humanitarian work.

Plant With Purpose was founded in 1984 by Tom Woodard, a San Diego businessman who had worked in the Dominican Republic as a relief volunteer following Hurricane David. He and his colleagues were frustrated that, although they were giving food to the poor, the root causes remained unaddressed. Day in and day out the same people required handouts to survive.

Instead of continuing to treat the symptom, Plant With Purpose followed the problem upstream, both literally and figuratively. The people were without food because deforestation made the land too poor to farm. The people themselves had caused much of the deforestation.

Forgotten People

Nearly one billion people make their livings as farmers at or near subsistence level. Since these men and women barely participate in the cash economy, they are overlooked by most economic indicators.

Urban poverty tends to get the most attention. It seems more ugly. The squalor of open sewers or the sight of children picking through smoldering garbage is shocking, whereas poor rural villages look quaint, peaceful, and bucolic.

But in many ways rural poverty is worse than urban poverty. Aid, opportunities, and services tend to be more available in the cities. Yet the rural poor make up almost 80 percent of the 840 million chronically hungry people in the world,[1] and the rural poor rank lower than the urban poor on almost every measure of human development.[2]

Although details vary depending on culture, climate, geography, ecology, and local markets, subsistence and near-subsistence farmers around the world have much in common in terms of lifestyle and the choices they are forced to make.[3] Since their reality is far removed from what we may be used to, a general description may be useful, keeping in mind that each situation will be different.

Land is scarce and severely degraded. The poor are left with the most marginal land: steep hillsides, rocky ravines, edges of forests, and the borders of national parks. Many families farm hillsides so steep that they are often injured falling out of their fields. Having gingerly made my way down some of those fields myself, I know how treacherous they can be.

A family of several generations might share a house of one or two rooms, typically with a dirt floor, some wooden chairs, a few plastic dishes, and one or two changes of clothes (often second-hand). Families may sleep on the floor or on wooden cots.

Most Dominican and Haitian houses are quite small, yet they are usually brightly painted in baby blue, pink, or green and decorated with ornate woodwork. Newer homes are made of cinderblock and have tin roofs, while older homes are wood.

Families tend to plant trees around their homes, for both shade and fruit.

Kitchens are usually in a nearby shack or shed, where the women cook over an open fire, breathing the smoke. In most places women are also responsible for gathering firewood and fetching water. These activities take up most of the day.

Running water and electricity are rare. Not all families have latrines, so human waste contaminates the local water supply.

Donated or resold clothes are everywhere and have destroyed local tailoring shops, while creating other industries. In the border region of Haiti where Plant With Purpose has its program, some families generate a modest income selling used shoes across the border. (Ironically, I have seen U.S. mission teams try to start income-generating sewing projects while simultaneously donating their own cast-offs to the same communities.)

Farmers frequently cultivate multiple small tracts of land several kilometers apart. A farmer might own a couple of plots, rent a few others, and sharecrop another. Much of the day is spent walking between fields. Hand tools such as picks, hoes, and machetes are used to work the rocky fields. Animals are rarely used.

I once spent an afternoon planting beans with some farmers in Haiti. Each of us carried a small sickle in one hand and bean seeds in the other. We dug through the rocks to make a small hole, dropped in a couple of seeds, and moved on. In short order, my hands started bleeding, my back ached, and I held out little hope for the beans I had planted. At least I had the comfort of knowing that I would be done in a few hours. For my friends in that field, this was daily life.

Educating children is one the most challenging expenses parents face. Children must have uniforms and pay school fees. The nearest school may be several kilometers away. Few young people attend more than a year or two. Most adults are illiterate.

Farmers have no bank accounts, so they prepare for emergencies by investing in livestock. Pigs, goats, and cows are viewed like insurance or savings.

Farmers eat a large percentage of what they grow, and they sell the surplus to buy cooking oil, rice, soap, and other necessities.

A family may generate income by selling produce or animals, or buying goods in the city and reselling them at the local market. Those who trade in goods from the urban areas rely on public transportation. In Haiti, that consists of enormous open trucks that ply the eroded dirt roads. Truck beds are filled with goods—charcoal, fruit, corn, animals, and produce. Dozens of people sit on top, cling to the sides, or ride on the front bumper. Many people make the trip on foot, pulling a donkey that carries everything they have to sell.

Diets are primarily beans, rice, and roots. A well-off family may eat three meals a day; in tougher times, only two. Meat is a luxury, eaten rarely.

Despite these hardships, visitors often remark on how happy these people seem to be. In Haiti, work is accompanied by motivational songs. There is a tradition of working cooperatively, sharing the labor on one another's farms. I have always been impressed by the sense of humor and the stoic perseverance of the Haitians.

Americans tend to have one of two equally inaccurate reactions to the poor. The first is to imagine poor people as helpless victims, and thus be surprised at their joy, intelligence, and abilities. Most short-term visitors have their stereotype of grim, downtrodden victims shattered by the reality of people with hopes, dreams, jokes, and compassion.

But this can often lead to the opposite reaction, which is to romanticize the poor. When speaking with first-time visitors to one of our programs, I often hear comments like "They are so much happier than we are" or "They don't even seem poor." This impression changes with a longer visit, as the reality is more complex. Alcoholism, domestic abuse, marital infidelity, petty crime, violence, and delinquency are common. The poor have the same character flaws and talents we have.

Causes of Deforestation

Among the many causes of widespread deforestation, cattle grazing and commercial logging are best known. Clearing of land for large-scale industrial agriculture is another. Because of the limited choices in where and how they can live, subsistence farmers are significant contributors as well.

In the Amazon, where more forest is lost than in any other place in the world, cattle ranching is the primary cause of deforestation. Ranching is responsible for 65–70 percent of deforestation, while small-holder agriculture (poor farmers) causes 20–25 percent.[4]

Worldwide, the numbers are different, with poor farmers causing an estimated 35–45 percent and cattle ranching 20–25 percent. Large-scale agriculture causes 15–20 percent, and logging is a distant forth with 10–15 percent.[5]

The poor contribute to deforestation in two principle ways: by cutting trees for timber or fuel (firewood and charcoal), and by clearing the forest to plant their crops.

In many parts of the world, firewood and charcoal are as important to the local economy as oil is to ours.[6] About 40 percent of the total energy requirement for Southeast Asia is met by wood fuels; in some Asian countries they provide more than 80 percent. In sub-Saharan Africa the numbers are even higher. In Congo, Ethiopia, and Tanzania, for example, the use of traditional wood fuels exceeds 90 percent.[7]

Some years ago I visited the tiny community of La Muralla, high in the pine forests of the Mixteca Alta in Oaxaca, Mexico. As I talked with the local mayor, I was shocked to learn that their only "cash crop"—the only source of income the community had—was charcoal. They used firewood for their own cooking and heating, but made charcoal to sell to those in the city.

Charcoal is made by baking wood in a kiln. It produces a cleaner and hotter burning fuel. In the cities of the developing world, huge markets sell bags of charcoal for use in the kitchens and homes of those who can afford it. Trucks stream out of the mountains and forests loaded with it, slowly converting the forest into smoke.

Near the mayor's office in La Muralla, a young family was making charcoal in a small clearing below the road. The entire family, including two small children about eight and five, bagged the product, their hands and faces covered in soot. They made a couple of hundred dollars per year this way—enough to buy a few items to supplement the corn and beans they grew for themselves.

For people with no other opportunities or resources, the forest becomes an emergency savings account. Charcoal production is one of the last options open for the poorest and most desperate, even in places where it is illegal. Some of the people we work with in the Dominican Republic have spent time in jail for charcoal production. But a parent will readily risk jail if it means being able to feed his or her children.

People often assume deforestation occurs because people don't know any better, but many poor farmers have a profound under-standing of how their land works. I have had Haitian and Domini-can farmers give me detailed descriptions of how a watershed functions. But Haitian farmers also have a proverb that says, "Either this tree must die, or I must die in its place."

Susan Stonich and Billie Dewalt, in a study on deforestation in Honduras, quote a Honduran farmer's eloquent explanation:

> I can only expect destruction for my family because I am provok-ing it with my own hands. This is what happens when the peas-ant doesn't receive help. . . . He looks for the obvious way out, which is to farm the mountain slopes and cut down the moun-tain vegetation. . . . I know what I am doing. . . . I am destroying the land.[8]

Years ago I heard of a farmer who, during a time of extended drought, became so desperate that he cut the fruit trees around his house to sell as firewood because he couldn't wait for the fruit to ripen. He clearly understood the stakes. The problem is not igno-rance, but a lack of opportunity and options.

Clearing land for small-scale agriculture is an even more impor-tant factor in deforestation than fuelwood. The practice of swid-den agriculture, sometimes called slash-and-burn farming, is often blamed. Swidden agriculture involves clearing the forest, burning the residue to release nutrients into the soil, farming for a couple of years, then moving on to new land when the soil is depleted. This age-old practice can be sustainable in the appropriate settings and conditions. Indeed, it has been practiced sustainably for millennia. Traditionally it was practiced with long fallow periods between plantings (where the land is left idle to regenerate), which allowed the forest to grow up again. However, population pressure and the use of marginal land upset this balance. When land is scarce, it is not left fallow long enough for the forest to regenerate. This is especially destructive when those without access to land that is more appropriate for farming cultivate steep hillsides that, once cleared of vegetation, quickly erode and become permanently degraded.

The inability of the poor to own their land or gain appropriate land tenure is another factor in its degradation. Squatters, sharecroppers, renters, and people who cannot gain legal title to their property have no long-term stake in the land, so they are unlikely to invest much in its future. In fact, for many, investing in the land could actually contribute to their losing it to covetous neighbors, landlords, or officials. No matter how well meaning a poor farmer might be, if he or she has no legal claim to the land, the economic incentives are against investing in its care. People tend to take care of what belongs to them.

The poor have no savings to fall back on, so the forest serves as their safety net. If there is a family emergency, the farmer responds by cutting a tree.

Yet we cannot lay the responsibility for the environmental crisis at the feet of the poor, the victims of environmental degradation who are forced by desperation, oppression, and lack of opportunities to abuse the environment. This is a vicious cycle in which they have little choice. Greed, exploitation, and carelessness on the part of governments, multinational corporations, businesses, and wealthy individuals are major contributors to the environmental crisis. And these people and organizations *do* have a choice.

Not many miles from La Muralla, there is another Mexican community, El Porvenir, which means "the future." When I first saw it, it was almost barren—in effect, a desert. Eroded hillsides were dusted with struggling patches of corn. Much of the region's income came from remittances from the United States, as there were few alternatives for income. The citizens of El Porvenir no longer had firewood and timber to sell. Making charcoal was not an option, and agriculture was marginal. This situation was a stark reminder of the potential future for the whole region.

Deforestation and Poverty

The most important assets a poor farmer has are the soil and water on the land he or she works. Soil and water are the wealth of the land, the basic building blocks for nutrition.

The great medical missionary Dr. Paul Brand points this out vividly in his essay "A Handful of Mud." In it he quotes an old Indian farmer, Tata, who, watching soil washing downstream, says:

> That mud flowing over the dam has given my family food since before I was born, and before my grandfather was born. It would have given my grandchildren and their grandchildren food forever. Now it will never feed us again. When you see mud in the channels of water, you know that life is flowing away from the mountains.[9]

God used Dr. Brand mightily to bless thousands of people. Among other achievements, he pioneered new techniques for fighting leprosy and wrote several books. Yet in spite of these contributions, he says:

> I would gladly give up medicine tomorrow if by so doing I could have some influence on policy with regard to mud and soil. The world will die from lack of pure water and soil long before it will die from a lack of antibiotics or surgical skill and knowledge.[10]

Emergency room physician Matthew Sleeth came to a similar conclusion a few years ago. He left his medical practice to devote himself full time to sharing the message of creation care and environmental stewardship to churches around the United States. Both Sleeth and Brand, doctors who had spent their lives treating the symptoms of environmental degradation, recognized the importance of a healthy environment and sought upstream solutions.

In a recent study David Pimentel reports that worldwide soil erosion rates are 10 to 40 times higher than replenishment rates. As a result nearly 30 percent of the world's arable land has become unproductive in the last forty years.[11]

Deforestation dramatically increases soil erosion. Tree roots hold the soil in place, while the forest canopy and leaf litter on the ground mitigate the impact of rain as it hits the soil, allowing it to soak in instead of running off. Studies have shown that 60 percent forest cover is necessary to prevent serious soil erosion,[12] and agricultural land experiences soil erosion at a rate about 75 times greater than forest land.[13] The steep slopes that the poor must often farm are even more vulnerable.

Eldon Garcia, Plant With Purpose's former director in the Dominican Republic, got started in the reforestation business as a government hydrologist seeking an antidote to erosion. He was concerned with how quickly silt—eroded soil—destroyed the usefulness of their hydroelectric dams.

Soil carried downstream eventually reaches the seas and becomes a hazard to fisheries and coral reefs. Aerial photos of places like Haiti and Madagascar show plumes of soil carried out to sea, destroying the life of the oceans.

On farms the poor struggle to grow crops without enough soil. In many places along the border between Haiti and the Dominican Republic, bare rock fills the fields.

Deforestation also dramatically impacts water availability and quality. Absence of trees results in a decrease in rainfall. Several studies have shown the important role of forests in recycling fresh water into the atmosphere through a process known as evapotranspiration.[14] Rather than entering the atmosphere locally, water runs off to the sea, affecting cloud formation.

Deforestation, leading to changes in precipitation, is believed to be one of the leading culprits in the melting glaciers of Kilimanjaro.[15] Elsewhere drought has increased and farmers who work without irrigation can no longer count on the regularity of rainfall.

It is tempting to think of deforestation in these far off continents as someone else's problem. But researchers have identified a connection between tropical deforestation and global rainfall patterns. A 2005 NASA study indicated that deforestation in the Amazon results in less rainfall in Texas and the Gulf of Mexico, whereas deforestation in Central Africa impacts rainfall in the U.S. Midwest. A combination of deforestation in both of these areas creates drought in California.[16] We are all connected by our dependence on the health of this planet.

Deforestation magnifies the problems caused by reduced rainfall. When rain does fall on deforested areas, there is little to stop it from running off before it can soak into the ground. Where the soil is protected by trees, the canopy breaks the fall of precipitation, leaf litter slows runoff, and roots increase soil permeability, so water is able to infiltrate and replenish local aquifers.

At a Vacation Bible School class, we illustrated this concept with two inclined tables representing hillsides. We placed large sponges on one table; the other was bare. Volunteers sat at the foot of the tables. We slowly poured water onto the tables. On the table with the sponges, the water was absorbed and the sponges stayed damp. On the other, the water ran down the table and poured into the volunteer's lap; no water remained on the table. Then we asked, "On which hillside would farmers most likely be able to grow food?" The answer was obvious.

Without infiltration, the aquifers are not recharged. Wells and springs run dry. Rivers that were once reliable sources of water flow only during heavy rains and then flood higher than in the past. Farmers spend hours every day carrying water from now-distant springs to their homes.

Trees also act as a filter. Studies have shown a direct correlation between the absence of forest cover and the presence of E. coli and other contaminants.[17] Healthy watersheds are so important to water quality, the City of New York invested $660 million in upstream land to protect its forests, thereby saving the $6 billion it would have cost to build an additional water purification plant.[18]

Lack of clean water is one of the biggest health hazards in the world today. As many as five thousand children die every day from waterborne illnesses.[19] Churches and humanitarian agencies have responded admirably to this need by drilling wells and providing water filtration or purification equipment. But few have followed the problem further upstream to the damaged watersheds where the problem originates.

Deforestation hurts us all, but especially the poor who cannot afford to have water piped into the home or to buy bottled water to drink. Instead, family members, mainly the women, walk hours to fetch water and the firewood necessary to boil it to make it safe to drink. As firewood becomes scarcer, costing more time and money, people are less likely to boil their water or adequately cook their food, compounding health risks and contributing to the downward cycle of desperation. Families who have no safety net are forced to take greater risks with their health and the well being of their families.

In addition to its impact on waterborne illness deforestation has numerous other negative health effects. Acute Lower Respiratory Infection is the leading killer of children under five and its incidence is dramatically increased by exposure to indoor cooking smoke.[20] There is also a correlation between deforestation and a number of infectious diseases. Recent studies show a direct link between malaria and deforestation.[21] In some locations deforestation has proved to be one of the most important variables in the incidence of leishmaniasis and hookworm.[22]

Catastrophic effects of deforestation include increased landslides and flooding. In 2004, massive flash floods along the Soliet River, caused in part by deforestation, raced through eastern Haiti, wiping out half of the community of Fonds Verrettes before arriving at the Dominican town of Jimani in the early dawn hours. A fifteen-foot-high wall of mud and boulders swept through the eastern part of this small border city, completely wiping that half of the city off the map and killing perhaps two thousand people. Similar floods have twice devastated the city of Gonaives in Haiti. Such tragedies are by no means isolated to Hispaniola. People die in floods and landslides around the world every year.

Hearkening back to our experiment with the table, even the biggest, most absorbent sponge wouldn't keep the person at the foot of the table dry if someone dumped the whole pitcher at once.

In the same way, there are some downpours that even the healthiest forests can't absorb. The floodwaters that raced through Jimani were produced when ten inches of rain fell in just twenty-four hours. No group of trees could have completely absorbed all that. Nonetheless, a healthy forest could have saved hundreds of lives, not to mention millions of dollars in relief aid and home-building projects.

Thankfully, many of these devastating processes are reversible. Just as deforestation robs people of their health and livelihood, reforestation and sustainable farming practices can begin to return it. This is a cycle we at Plant With Purpose have been fortunate to begin to see.

CHAPTER 3

Reversing the Cycle

In December 1997 Plant With Purpose's technical director, Bob Morikawa, and our new Haitian director, Jean-Mari Desilus (whom we called Dezo), traveled with me to the Haitian village of Kavanac. The sun beat down on us as we walked a steep, narrow path between hillside farms, their tiny fields separated from one another by loose rock walls. Ragged corn struggled through the rocks on either side of us. My lunch was not sitting well.

After we'd crossed one ridge and were on our way up a second long slope, I told the others I needed a rest. As I sat on a large stone, contemplating the hill in front of me, two elderly women came up the hill, five-gallon buckets of water balanced on their heads. *"Bon swa, blan,"* they greeted me. They asked where we were going, and Dezo told them we were headed to a village meeting in Kavanac. The older woman said they were on their way to the same meeting. "We'll let them know you will be along in a while," she said with a teasing grin.

At the top of the last ridge, I could see the Caribbean to the south, Haiti's tallest mountain, Pic La Selle, shrouded in clouds to the east, and the brilliant blue water of the Bay of Port-au-Prince to the north. A little farther along the ridge sat a group of about forty farmers, men and women, in an open-sided lean-to made of wood and corrugated tin. When we reached them, several sidled up to me and discreetly held out their hands while rubbing their stomachs.

I shook my head, indicating I had nothing to give them.

The meeting convened and moved past pleasantries to a series of questions from the community as to what Plant With Purpose intended to do in the village. A woman stood and, in a confrontational tone, told me about the other humanitarian agencies that had worked in the area. She named two agencies that had brought food and clothes, then left and never returned. "How is Plant With Purpose going to be any different?"

After giving the question some consideration, I responded, "Well, first of all, we are not going to give you anything."

She looked stunned.

"Second, we are not going to leave until you ask us to."

The woman stood there, speechless.

Once we understand God's heart for justice and the vicious cycle of deforestation and poverty that traps the poor, how do we respond? The desire to help is admirable in a world where far too many pass by on the other side of the road. But determining how to respond can be complicated.

I was originally drawn to the work of serving the poor and hungry because it seemed simple, unambiguous, and virtuous. I had studied political science and was often struck by the moral ambiguity and unexpected consequences of most policy choices. Well-intended programs often had the opposite effect of what their drafters expected. The most well-meaning projects could cause great harm. As I was to discover, humanitarian work can be nearly as complicated.

Many humanitarian organizations respond to poverty and injustice by giving surplus food, medicine, and clothes, and maybe starting orphanages and clinics. They focus on treating the symptoms of poverty—which sorely need to be treated. But others ask questions about the root causes: Why are people are hungry and sick? Why so many orphaned children?

The Bible seems pretty straightforward in its approach: give a cup of cold water in the name of the Lord. Our first response is often to give things away. The poor clearly lack things, and we have things, so what could be more obvious than giving out of our abundance?

Yet giving things often comes with unintended consequences. Without knowing the needs and challenges faced by local communities, our gifts can be inappropriate. In one community where we work, a relatively new bulldozer sat in front of a school yard for many years, slowly rusting. No doubt it was given with the best of intentions and was probably very expensive to ship. Yet it was completely inappropriate to the local conditions. It ended up serving as a germination bed for weeds and a few small trees before being sold for scrap.

Even when gifts are appropriate to the needs of the people, they can often create dependency. Haiti has received numerous donations and many short-term mission teams have come to share the gospel and build churches and school buildings. Yet there is a growing school of thought that much of our aid may be hurting the locals.

As we were establishing Plant With Purpose in Haiti, a long-time missionary sternly informed us that he wasn't sure Haiti needed another well-intended nonprofit agency. "We have created a nation of beggars," he said. "For years folks have been coming down here thinking they are helping by giving things away. But that just teaches people to beg." Another missionary told me that after citizens in one village received cracked wheat from USAID, few local farmers bothered to plant corn because they couldn't compete with free food.

Often, the problem is less with aid itself than with how it is applied. We tend to focus on short-term, immediate-impact solutions rather than long-term investments in people. Many Americans have at least a passing understanding of what handouts do to initiative, self-esteem, and motivation. We talk of how a welfare mentality creates dependency. When we see panhandlers on the street corner, most of us realize a handout won't change their lives. A gospel tract probably won't do much good, either—

though it may be better than handing them a dollar. Unfortunately, we don't always translate that understanding into our approach to the poor overseas.

Talents

An insight from Scripture comes in the parable of talents in Matthew 25:14-30. The man who received five talents put it to work and made five more; the man given two talents made two more. The individual who received only one talent buried it. Most sermons preached on this passage emphasize the need to utilize what God has given us. And that is an important lesson.

But there is something odd about the ending of the parable. The poorest man, the one who is given the least yet fails to take advantage of what he has, is thrown into the outer darkness. It has always struck me as strange that the poor man is the bad guy in this story.

Jesus could have conveyed the same message about using what we've been given if the man who received two talents were the one who buried them. Or he could have made the man receiving five talents the unfaithful one, which would seem in keeping with his other warnings to the rich. But for some reason he chose to make an example of the "one-talent man."

For the time being I have given up trying to decipher the justice of the parable. But I have come to realize that, fair or not, it actually fits my real-life experience. The poor are often unaware of their own talents, resources, and power. They have been labeled as helpless, backwards, and uneducated so often that they have begun to believe it. They have, in effect, buried their talents.

Just as the man in the parable believed a lie about the character of the master, many of the people we work with have come to believe a lie about who God is, about their relationship with him, and about what they have been given. Though many of them are Christians, they often believe they have little to offer.

When Jesus told the parable, one talent was worth a significant amount of money, so in fact the "one-talent man" was not actually poor. Similarly, the gifts that God has given to every one of us—even the poorest of the poor—are of immense value when put to use.

One evening in the early days of our work in Haiti, several of us sat on the front porch of a guesthouse in Grand Colline, exchanging stories and watching fireflies. Pere Albert, the Haitian Episcopal priest with whom we partnered, came up the path from the vocational school building, where he lived, to join us.

The conversation turned to his testimony. He told us how happy he was that God had given him a task to do. "God gives each of us something to do for him," he said. "It's as if a boss gathered together a group of his workers, and he turned to each one and said, 'I have a very important job for you.'" With childlike glee he exclaimed, "It makes me happy that God wants to work with me. I feel excited!"

Then he asked, "Can you imagine how you'd feel if, when the boss got to you, he skipped you because he had nothing for you to do?"

For the first time, it dawned on me how terrible it must feel to believe you have nothing to contribute, to feel you are and always will be completely dependent on the goodwill of outsiders. The good news, implicit in the Mathew 25 parable, is that everyone has been given talents they can work with. We all have something to contribute to the kingdom of God. Each of us has an important role to play. This is news we need to hear for ourselves and share with others, because it is significant and too often neglected.

The lie of the world, reinforced by the media and believed by millions, is that the poor are worthless. The global economic system measures worth in dollars—you are paid according to how society values your contribution. The message is that as a Haitian farmer, no matter how bright you are, and no matter how hard you work, you will never be worth more than a few hundred dollars a year.

We need to defeat the lie that says worth is measured in dollars.

Sadly, the poor and many of those who try to help them have unknowingly bought into this lie. For the poor, it is manifested in a lack of self-confidence, self-esteem, and initiative. For those seeking to help, it manifests itself in condescension and patronizing attitudes.

Empowerment and Transformation

I was in Chicago to attend a conference, and I decided to visit my former church. When I contacted the present pastor for his permission, he not only gave it but also promised to gather some of my former parishioners.

As I started up the street toward my old church, I was astounded by the changes in my old neighborhood. No more trash lay in the gutters, trees were flourishing along the once-barren street, new sidewalks had been laid, the businesses were obviously thriving, lawns in front of apartment buildings lay green and verdant, and apartments were painted and pointed. "This community no longer belongs to the poor," I thought. "It has been gentrified!"

How wrong I was.

When I got to the church and greeted my former members, one woman who had been part of our community organizing effort asked, "Well, what do you think of your old neighborhood?"

"I'm blown away," I responded. "What happened?"

I was thrilled by what she told me. That neighborhood hadn't been gentrified at all. Instead, the community organization I'd helped found had pulled together the shops, businesses, churches, and the residents to reclaim that neighborhood. Those citizens had organized to push out the criminal element and to rebuild their neighborhood, by providing their own volunteer sweat and pressuring the city to bring in funding to renovate it. The people insisted that such renovation had to be green.

The interests of each person and every group in the community had been served, not by seeking anyone's individual good but by organizing together to seek the community's good. Thus, what had been a former slum had become a delightful place to live— because the members of that community were willing to use the significant people-power at their disposal.

Dr. Robert C. Linthicum is founder and president emeritus of Partners in Urban Transformation.

Unfortunately, when outsiders offer help, whether through foreign aid, short-term missions, or donations, we often reinforce this lie. We bring used clothes that put local tailors out of business and give away free food that undercuts the local farmers. We construct buildings for people, putting local masons and carpenters out of work and implicitly sending the message that it takes outsiders to get things done. We may even encourage small businesses based on models that work in the United States, but because we don't understand the culture and local economics, these businesses fail. And that failure reinforces the lie that the local people are incapable of succeeding.

The elders from an evangelical church in a small village in Mexico approached me about the construction of a new church building. A concrete foundation had been poured, and had been sitting there for years. When I asked why they'd not started building it, one of the elders told me, "We have been waiting for you to come do it for us."

I don't mean to disparage anyone who gives to the poor. We are commanded to do so. There are times when a handout is the most important thing a person can receive. People need assistance when they are sick, or after a disaster, or helpless. Children who have no families clearly need someone to care for them.

But if we do for others what they can and should do for themselves, we rob them of their dignity and reinforce the lie that they have nothing to offer. We create dependency.

A story is told of travelers who come into a community during a famine and ask for something to eat. They are told there is nothing. The travelers take out a pot and begin to make soup by boiling some stones. When asked about it, they explain that they are making "stone soup" and only need a bit of garnish to improve it. One by one everyone in the village brings something to contribute. In the end a fine stew is made, with everyone eating their fill.

Similarly, the members of a community often have the materials and resources needed to change their situation. Sometimes people just need a catalyst and a little organization to create something far better than any of them could have imagined.

To minimize the sense of dependence on outsiders, Plant With Purpose works through indigenous partner organizations, staffed by local directors and teams. These indigenous leaders have taught me a great deal.

In Haiti, Dezo stressed time and again that we must not give things away, because the "peasants" weren't helpless. In Mexico, I learned the importance of community participation and ownership. In Tanzania I discovered the significance of responding to community priorities. If we come in with our preconceived notions of what needs to be fixed, we inevitably fail.

This is a difficult lesson for Americans to learn, coming from our take-charge, can-do culture. Even when we understand our tendency to take charge, it is difficult for us to resist. Bryant Myers, in *Walking with the Poor,* talks about the temptation to play God in the lives of the poor.[1] We want to be heroes when that is not rightfully our role. The temptation to be "like God" led to the downfall of Adam and Eve, and it remains strong today.

The first step in our work is helping people understand their own power and their value in the kingdom. This is foundational. However, empowerment takes time. It requires patience and the participation of the local people. We need to get over our American tendency to be task-oriented and to think we know all the answers. The local people must take responsibility for the change they want to see in their communities. They need to participate in and own the plan. There are a host of participatory tools for making this happen.

When it comes to solving the problem of poverty, the poor themselves are our most important allies, yet they are probably the most overlooked. When it comes to issues of rural environmental degradation, the rural poor have the skills, insight, and vested interest to solve these problems. They have far more intelligence and initiative than most people give them credit for. Sometimes all they lack is self-confidence or opportunity.

Yet far too often, those who want to help view the poor as an obstacle. The temptation is to try to solve their problems for them without involving them. One of the most important things we can do is empower the poor to realize and use their God-given talents to change their communities and restore their land.

Rather than doing the projects ourselves, we outsiders need to facilitate the process. Only after the local community identifies what is holding them back, the barriers to their progress, should we step in with what we can contribute. Too many times, I have seen this process reversed.

If you are giving things away, a poor community will almost always accept your donations, no matter how inappropriate. Even if you don't offer input up front, they may try to anticipate what it is you have to give away and match their needs to that.

There are a number of biblical examples of people being empowered to participate in their own development. For example, Boaz saw Ruth and took pity on her and her mother-in-law. But rather than simply offering her charity, he let her glean in his fields, preserving her dignity and giving her an opportunity to work.

Another interesting example is seen in the feeding of the five thousand. The disciples told Jesus the crowd was hungry. He could have responded in myriad ways, immediately providing the people with food. But his first response to the disciples was to tell them to feed the people. "You give them something to eat," he said (Mark 6:37). Jesus used what they could contribute as the starting point for a miracle. Stone soup plus the divine hand of God.

Unless we get to know people as individuals, we cannot know what will change their lives. If we don't invest ourselves in their lives, we won't be aware of what they need. When Jesus first sent his disciples out, he told them to take nothing and to depend on the local people for hospitality. By depending on the local people, the disciples formed a deeper connection, getting to know the people to whom they were ministering. This was the first short-term mission.

The relationships the disciples formed as they went out were much more equitable than those formed on most mission trips. In fact, our short-term teams are usually so laden with used clothes, surplus medicine, give-away items, and extras for our own comfort, moving the team to the field sometimes requires extra vehicles. Yet it is only when a real relationship is established that the good news of the kingdom can be shared.

Act as if . . .

God's kingdom is a mystery in many ways: at once within us and coming; now and future. The concept was confusing to the disciples even though they had the benefit of being mentored daily by the very Author of the kingdom, so it is small wonder that the idea of the kingdom is confusing to us. We tend to over-spiritualize it, or confuse it with our own nationalistic conceits, or try to build it on our own, creating some sort of earthly utopia. These efforts almost always turn out badly. But we can model kingdom-type relationships in our work and in our programs. We can live as if we are already in the kingdom.

Our board chairman, a successful businessman, used to coach me to "act as if." Act as if Plant With Purpose were already the organization we wanted it to be. Act as if we had the resources, reputation, and talent to be the best. His point was not to misrepresent ourselves, but rather that our actions become a self-fulfilling prophecy.

Jesus tells us to practice the same in relationship to the kingdom. We can act as if our lives are rooted in the teachings of God's kingdom. We can act as if it makes sense to turn the other cheek, to give away a shirt if someone asks us for a coat, to act as if we love our enemies and can trust our neighbors. We can act as if the curse has been lifted.

In Genesis 3:17-19 we read of this curse:

> Cursed is the ground because of you; through painful toil you will eat of it all the days of your life. . . . It will produce thorns and thistles for you. . . . By the sweat of your brow you will eat your food.

The Scripture also speaks of a day when the curse laid upon the ground for Adam's sin will be a distant memory. Looking forward to that day, we can act as if we were working *with* creation instead of against it.

Ultimately, the curse has already been broken through Christ's work on the cross, yet we still live with its effects. Though we cannot create the kingdom, we can proclaim it and model it in our actions and relationships, including our relationship with creation. By so doing, we can begin to reverse vicious cycles, such as the cycle of deforestation and poverty.

From Vicious Cycles to Victorious Cycles

We have the opportunity to begin to transform these vicious cycles into virtuous cycles, where each change makes the next change more effective. A vicious cycle of deforestation and poverty can become a virtuous cycle of reforestation and economic empowerment. When the Holy Spirit is involved and kingdom relationships are modeled, a virtuous cycle can become a victorious cycle.

A virtuous cycle is created when we make environmental restoration profitable for the rural poor at the same time as we make poverty-reduction beneficial for the environment. The problems of deforestation and poverty, when taken by themselves, seem intractable. If you address only one of them, either the environmental or the economic, the one you ignore will beat you. However, when addressed together the solutions can be mutually reinforcing.

One of Plant With Purpose's key principles is that it is easier to address both problems together than to take on each one individually. Thus we simultaneously emphasize environmental and economic solutions.

But there is also a spiritual dimension to these problems. For lasting change to take place, we believe Jesus must be involved. We cannot succeed in our task unless Jesus empowers us and walks with us. In order for lives to be transformed, Christ must be working in people's lives.

That is not to say we force our faith or our witness on anyone. We serve the poor out of our love for Jesus, and it is our desire that people would come to know him, but we do not want to manipulate people in any way. To imply in any way that someone needs to convert in order to receive help from Plant With Purpose would be manipulative, so we go out of our way to make it clear to people that their involvement in the spiritual activities of Plant With Purpose is optional. Yet we believe only Jesus can take a virtuous cycle of economic opportunity and environmental restoration and turn it into something that truly resembles the kingdom of God— a victorious cycle.

We work to create virtuous cycles where economic development, environmental restoration, and discipleship intersect. We begin by empowering the poor to make their own choices. It is the basis for everything else we try to do, including sharing the good news.

Back to Kavanac

After that first meeting in Kavanac in 1997, Dezo and our local staff began getting together with the farmers group on a regular basis. The staff facilitated planning, provided training, and organized a loan group.

Three years later, I again made the trek up the stony ridges to the tiny meeting house on the spine of Haiti's southern peninsula. This time I was met by a very different group. No one asked me for money. Everyone was eager to tell me all they had accomplished. A credit group had been formed and members were receiving loans. Trees had been planted. Rainwater harvesting systems and cisterns had been constructed. Families were buying land they had formerly rented or sharecropped. Fruit trees had been made more productive through grafting.

The highlight of the meeting occurred when a woman I knew as Madan (Creole for *Mrs.*) Forvil stood up and proudly said, "What you have given us is the knowledge that we are not helpless, but that God has given us talents we can use to change our community."

Seeing those talents emerge was exciting for me. The dejected group I'd met in 1997 turned out to be an extraordinarily gifted community. I often wonder what they could have done had they been given the opportunities so many of us take for granted and even squander.

The story of Kavanac has not been 100 percent smooth or successful. And it is not finished. But the first and most important steps have been taken. And we can be certain that transformation will continue long after we leave.

CHAPTER 4

Sustainable Agriculture and Forestry

I spent the morning in a long-tailed boat with Rick Burnette and Jamlong, both of whom work with Plant With Purpose's Thai partner, UHDP. The three of us motored up the chocolate-colored river through a continuous drizzle. Then we hiked through several Lahu villages and waded into a densely forested valley. Green rice paddies were the only sign of human presence. Mud sucked at the two-dollar rubber boots I'd bought in the market that morning to save my expensive hiking boots.

We trudged up a hill, and at the top we came upon a dozen wooden and bamboo houses on stilts. Jamlong led Rick and me up the stairs of the nearest house. We were greeted by Uncle Tisae, a wizened old pipe-smoking Lahu man with a brimless cap and a glint in his eye. Uncle Tisae invited us to sit on the floor while he prepared tea over an open fire. After much joking conversation with Jamlong, which was not translated and often drowned out by the pounding of the rain, Uncle Tisae took us outside to see his forest garden.

Many American visitors to Plant With Purpose farms mistake banana, cacao, or coffee plantations for rainforest. I considered myself a bit more sophisticated than that, so I was surprised to learn that the dense and diverse forest we were climbing through had been intentionally planted by Tisae a few years earlier on a barren hillside that had once held dryland rice. As we scrambled through tangled undergrowth, Tisae handed me fruits, berries, twigs, and leaves to eat or chew. Some I recognized, such as jackfruit and tea leaves. Others I had never seen. Even the things we couldn't eat had been intentionally planted for the products they could provide.

This hillside land had been eroded to the point where it was considered unproductive. But now it provided Tisae with a sustainable source of food and income, and he was teaching others to farm in a similar way. This complex agroforestry system represented one of many creative ways to restore areas that might seem depleted.

When Americans think of agriculture, images of large, flat expanses and big farm machinery usually come to mind. In much of the developing world, the reality couldn't be more different. Machinery and chemicals are both expensive and ill-suited to the land farmed by many poor people throughout the world. However, there is a host of techniques that will increase yields and sustainability in these conditions.

One of the overwhelming lessons I've learned is the incredible diversity and provision of creation. God has given us many ways to grow food.

Agroforestry

One alternative farming method is agroforestry. This term includes a wide range of techniques that incorporate trees into farming systems in order to take advantage of the unique interactions that occur. Such methods have been practiced for centuries around the world, but agroforestry has gained a great deal of attention in the past couple of decades.

Far more sustainable than many other methods of farming, agroforestry allows a farmer to cultivate the same plot of land indefinitely. The trees on a farm can provide many of the ecosystem services of the native forest—helping the watershed function more naturally, improving soil ecology, and increasing local biodiversity.

Agroforestry is particularly well suited to steep, eroded hillsides. Trees help stabilize the soil and can be incorporated into barriers that control erosion. They also provide organic matter in the form of leaves and root dieback, which helps improve soil health and fertility. Because they send roots deeper than many annual crops, trees can access water and nutrient resources that would otherwise be unavailable, bringing them to the surface where they can be utilized by other crops. The idea is to maximize positive interactions between trees and crops, while minimizing negative interactions such as competition for sunlight, water, or nutrients.

One of the prominent interactions utilized in many agroforestry systems involves trees or shrubs that "fix" nitrogen. Many trees, especially legumes, can, through an interaction with bacteria on their roots, "fix" the atmospheric nitrogen in the soil, thereby contributing to soil fertility. Thus the tree becomes a source of organic fertilizer for annual crops. It also provides shade, screens weaker plants from wind, and repels pests.

The more common agroforestry systems include:[1]

- Improved fallows: intentionally planting leguminous trees on land that is otherwise idle, between plantings of annual crops.
- Taungya: combining annual or perennial crops with trees in the early stages of establishing a tree plantation.
- Alley cropping: planting trees in rows or hedges separated by strips of annual crops. Trees provide a living barrier, reducing soil erosion and providing animal fodder and organic fertilizer in the form of leaves harvested from the hedgerows.
- Home gardens: systems that include diverse species of trees planted around the home. These are often arranged in a "multi-story" fashion, taking advantage of vertical space to grow several products. The Chagga people, whom Plant With Purpose works with in Tanzania, have utilized a complex multi-story home garden consisting of root crops such as taro at the lowest level, with shade-grown coffee at the intermediate level, and fruit and timber trees at the highest level.

Other classifications of agroforestry include systems that combine trees with pastures or fish farms. A common system in the Caribbean includes the use of nitrogen-fixing trees as living fence posts.

One of the first models we used in the Dominican Republic included a three-to-four acre woodlot (a grove of trees planted for timber or firewood) in tandem with about three acres of oregano and citrus trees. On Plant With Purpose farms the woodlot was planted with fast-growing trees, often eucalyptus or *Acacia mangium,* and was grown expressly for harvest, as one might grow corn. Poles for construction can be produced from this system in two or three years, and timber can be ready for harvest in seven-to-ten years. Many of the farmers we worked with in the Dominican Republic had relatively abundant land, although it was significantly degraded. Since trees will grow on steep and degraded hillsides, the woodlot was a perfect use for it.

While the woodlot offered a stable source of longer-term income, the oregano and citrus trees provided short-term income. Oregano, a traditional cash crop in the area, could be turned around in just a few months. This gave income to the farmers while the trees matured. This portion of the farm was intercropped with citrus trees: oranges, mandarins, and limes, usually surrounded with living fence posts. A number of other short-term crops were used—among them peppers, cilantro, and annatto—but the focus was on oregano and wood.

The technical assistance we provided allowed the farmers to get better-quality oregano, which sold at a higher price. As a result, interest in the crop grew, and before long everyone was growing oregano. Predictably, the oregano market abruptly collapsed, leaving farmers with a glut of oregano. We had our first lesson in the volatility of agricultural markets and learned the danger of relying on a single product, rather than minimizing risk by diversification.

We were also reminded of one reason we must empower people to make their own decisions. I once sat in on a meeting between about 120 farmers and our Dominican staff and board, during which farmer after farmer told us of their dashed hopes. They had done everything we had suggested, only to have crops that were worth less than what they had cost to produce. "You told us to do this, and now look where we are."

The Good Steward

Good stewards return the gifts of creation with gifts of their own. A good steward is a "caretaker," not just a "taker." The good steward is a planter of trees, not merely a cutter of trees.

The good steward:

1. works to maintain and foster a vibrant human community within creation's economy;
2. works to behold, restore, and maintain God's provisions for the creation in forest and field;
3. observes responses of the land and its ecosystems to changes made by caring and uncaring people;
4. works to counter degradation of land and life by restoring and maintaining the land, the soil, and its living creatures;
5. seeks to learn from the good and bad practices of other people, both locally and regionally; and
6. reflects God's care and love for the world in all that he or she does.

The essence of stewardship is fostering human community while at the same time fostering the living world that sustains life on earth. This means, for example, that in working to achieve increased food production, the good steward does not respond to soil loss and decline of soil fertility simply by adding still more chemicals. Instead, the good steward strives to understand the processes of soil formation and fertility in order to do things that restore soils in harmony with their native ecological systems.

Good stewards continue to observe and study the consequences of their actions and inactions, so that both the food plants and the ecosystem continue to flourish.

Dr. Calvin DeWitt is the founding director of the Au Sable Institute of Environmental Studies and a professor at the Nelson Institute for Environmental Studies, University of Wisconsin–Madison.

Further down the road, however, the woodlots proved to be successful. The market for eucalyptus poles and posts far exceeded our expectations, and farmers learned to do their own marketing. Several of the villages in which we worked are now thriving middle-class communities with comfortable homes.

Eucalyptus coppices well (that is, it resprouts from a cut stump), so trees planted twenty years ago are still growing, even though they may have been cut and sold three or four times. Initial success with eucalyptus and acacia helped farmers take a longer view and diversify their planting to include slower-growing but higher-value species, including pine and mahogany.

In general, we advocate for native species; however, Dominican farmers value exotic species, like eucalyptus, for their fast-growing characteristics and ready market. These trees are grown as a cash crop rather than for reforestation. Environmentally, it is an intermediate step—slowing deforestation by eliminating the need for farmers to practice swidden agriculture and by providing products that would otherwise come from the native forest. It also provides some of the ecological services a native forest would provide, but it is not restoration of native forest. Many agroforestry systems rely on fast-growing multipurpose tree species from Southeast Asia. Many of these trees have wonderful properties and are highly valued by farmers. However, more research needs to be done on the properties of native species and their applicability to agroforestry systems.

When we began, cutting trees had been illegal in the Dominican Republic for many years. These laws slowed deforestation, but they also removed the incentive to plant trees, because farmers could not benefit from them. Thus it was necessary to advocate for the right of farmers to harvest trees they had planted.

If farmers are given the right to benefit from the trees and see a return on them, they are more willing to plant and nurture them. Making it legal to cut what one plants helps put market incentives to work on behalf of tree planting. Plant With Purpose operates a couple of small sawmills to help farmers bring their products to market.

This is not the only example of well-intended environmental laws having unintended consequences. In Southeast Asia, farmers have indicated a reluctance to plant too many trees or develop too much diversity in their forest gardens, lest the government declare the forest a natural reserve and no longer allow access.

The agroforestry systems in the Dominican Republic are relatively simple, utilizing only a couple of species in combination. But we have worked with more complex systems with many species. Uncle Tisae's farm uses of a diverse variety of native forest species along with non-native cash crops. In many of these forest gardens, the untrained eye would have a hard time distinguishing between native forest and cultivated agroforestry.

Many agencies have effectively used agroforestry systems to increase income and sustainability, and to restore the land. World Vision, for example, has implemented large-scale agroforestry programs in Ethiopia, Zambia, Niger, and the Philippines.[2] The Zambian program saw large increases in yields and sustainability, and ultimately reached far more people than initially targeted as neighboring farmers recognized the value of agroforestry and readily adopted the techniques.[3]

As Plant With Purpose grew, we learned that agroforestry is not applicable to every setting. It is one of many tools that can be employed to help the poor and their environment. We once defined ourselves by our tools rather than our outcomes, thinking of ourselves as an "agroforestry organization." However, if your goal is to build houses, defining yourself as a "hammer operator" is debilitating.

When we placed emphasis on our desired outcome of reversing deforestation and poverty, we were free to analyze what tools were most useful in achieving those goals.[4] We found that agroforestry was an important and useful tool, but not the only tool we would employ. Branching out from our work in agroforestry, which lies at the intersection of forestry and agriculture, we moved into community forestry and sustainable agriculture.

Sustainable Agriculture

We live in a time when most of the world looks down upon farming and especially small farmers. Once upon a time, the idea of owning your own farm and being self-sufficient was highly prized in America. However, with mechanized agriculture that relies on chemical inputs, the modern farm is more like a factory. Nonetheless, in the mountainous regions where Plant With Purpose works, small-scale hillside farming is probably the only type of farming that will ever be done. The areas simply don't lend themselves to mechanized farming.

In these countries, detaching 98 percent of the population from the land, as we have done in the United States, will not work. However, our culture has a profound influence on the rest of the world, and our attitudes carry over into the capitals of the developing world. While small business is highly prized, small-scale farmers are seen as backward, holding back the progress of the nation. Even some of our donors see small-business creation and getting people off the farm as one of the best things we can offer. But small-scale farming can be a viable solution when it is practiced in a sustainable way so it provides for the families who depend on it.

In some of our programs, we use a curriculum developed by David Evans of Food for the Hungry. It points out that God is the original farmer, the one who planted the first garden and created the incredible variety of plants and animals we have available for our food. It also reminds farmers that agriculture is a high calling.[5]

Small farmers are a vital part of the future. Migration off the farm and into the overcrowded cities of the developing world, where unemployment rates skyrocket, is ultimately unsustainable. Granted, some of this migration occurs because there is not enough land. Land that has been divided among heirs for generations can no longer be effectively subdivided, and some must find other employment. But when they arrive in the cities, many find that their perceived opportunities don't exist.

For example, some estimates place the unemployment rate in Port-au-Prince at 70 percent. It would take hundreds of thousands of new jobs to even begin to make a dent.[6] Furthermore, for every new job created in the city, additional job seekers are drawn in from the country, exacerbating urban unemployment.[7] In countries where food security is a problem, sustainable, productive small-scale agriculture is vital.

Even in the United States, there is a strong movement toward small-scale local agriculture. High-input industrial monocultures are showing signs of being unsustainable while producing an inferior product. As public awareness grows, more people are turning to alternative sources, such as Community Supported Agriculture (CSA). In a CSA, individual consumers buy shares in a local farm, which distributes a percentage of the week's produce to the shareholders. Shareholders get what the farm grows, participating in its abundance, scarcity, and seasonality. At the same time, the farmers have an incentive to cultivate a diversity of crops, which is better for the land. This aspect of the local food movement is a small step toward bridging the gap between farmer and eater in the United States.

Plant With Purpose uses and teaches a number of sustainable agriculture techniques tailored to local environments, including cover crops, bio-intensive vegetable gardens, zero-till systems, seed selection, soil conservation, natural pest control, organic farming, fish farming, and animal husbandry. Where villages have access to significant natural forest resources, we teach and support sustainable forestry management.

Each method has its adherents and advocates. One method popular with some Christian agencies is called Farming God's Way. This is a conservation farming technique in which crop residues are left behind without burning or plowing.[8] It emphasizes precision in planting and high standards in weeding, as well as a number of scriptural principles such as tithing and working with joy. This method was originally developed for large-scale agriculture and has been used in Zimbabwe for many years.

Others agencies promote a wide range of sustainable agricultural practices including permaculture, agroecology, Holistic Management, and other systems in which natural closed-loop processes are mimicked. A host of resources on sustainable agriculture systems is available online. In addition, several institutions exist to provide information and instruction to nonexperts. Of these Plant With Purpose has worked most closely with ECHO (Educational Concerns for Hunger Organization),[9] and strongly recommends their services. Operating out of an experimental farm in North Fort Myers, Florida, ECHO networks agricultural missionaries and small-scale agricultural workers around the world, hosts annual conferences, publishes a helpful newsletter, and offers an excellent internship program.

One thing common to all sustainable systems is that each one of them, to one degree or another, copies the cycles of nature. We can only speculate what creation in a pre-fall world must have been like, yet for all that has been tainted and degraded by the curse and our sin, the beauty of the way God created the world is evident everywhere. Scripture tells us that God works everything together for good, and that he brings life from death. These truths are obvious in the intricate ways ecosystems fit together. Nothing is wasted, and everything has its niche. Everywhere, resurrection is foreshadowed and life springs forth from death. Time and again we see virtuous cycles.

On the other hand, with modern mechanized agriculture and the use of chemical fertilizers and pesticides, waste is not reused. In the United States, government subsidies for corn have led to the removal of animals from farms, thus creating, as Wendell Berry says, two problems (waste and lack of fertility) from one solution.[10] For poor farmers, who cannot afford the expensive inputs that sustain Western agriculture, it is important that we seek out the solutions God has already provided. Working with creation rather than against it, learning from these cycles, and wasting as little as possible, we can bring life from death.

For these farmers, organic farming is much more than a marketing gimmick. It is better for the environment, much less expensive when all the costs are considered, and far more sustainable in fragile ecosystems. Organic agriculture recognizes that farming is complex, and that local farmers, with their intimate knowledge of their own land, know best how to solve their particular problems. Thus, the methods evolve to match the local environment. Building on local knowledge, organic agriculture can revitalize traditional customs and encourage local self-reliance (and self-confidence), contributing to the ongoing process of empowerment.

There is a tremendous need for innovation and continuous research in farming. As development expert Roland Bunch said, "We are not here to develop their agriculture, but to teach them a way in which they can develop their own agriculture."[11] With that in mind, Plant With Purpose has resisted the adoption of a single system, but rather draws on all of them. Studies are conducted on small-farm research centers, where innovations from formal research institutions are tried out in a local context, while farmers are encouraged to conduct trials and experiments of their own design.

Community Forestry

Plant With Purpose promotes watershed restoration via community forestry. Large-scale reforestation projects are usually unsuccessful unless the local community takes ownership of the process. The natural desire as an outsider is to come in and plant trees on a massive scale, but without community participation, these trees will be turned into next year's charcoal or firewood supply or simply die of neglect. The program is only likely to succeed if the community sees a clear benefit from keeping trees in place.

These projects are challenging because the benefits for a community are long term and dispersed, making it difficult to create incentives for reforestation. Nonetheless, over the last twenty years we have seen tremendous results, with millions of trees surviving. In a couple of locations, streams that had become seasonal with very irregular flow became full, clear, and regular once again, serving as the primary water source for local communities.

In Haiti, where the intensity of cultivation is high and land ownership fragmented, we gathered coalitions of land owners in key micro-watersheds, encouraging them to work together to reforest and implement soil-conservation measures. Unless land owners can work together, individual efforts are in vain.

After being struck by four major tropical storms in a three-week period in late 2008, interest in this program grew dramatically. People saw firsthand how much better the land treated with soil-conservation measures survived compared with untreated land.

Sanitation, Animals, and a Healthy Ecosystem

Sanitation is a huge and unappreciated problem. In rural villages human waste goes directly into the rivers and streams, contributing to the toll of diarrheal illness. Ordinary latrines are a step up, but waste still leaches into the ground water. Composting latrines offer a better solution—one that makes far more sense than our own system of using fresh water to flush our waste into the sea.

A composting latrine has a chamber enclosed in concrete, keeping waste out of the ground water. The models we construct have two sides, each with its own seat and chamber. One side is used for six months, and then closed off while the other side is used. A shunt in the toilet separates liquid and solid. Urine is diluted and used as fertilizer.

The solid waste is kept dry and allowed to compost over the six months the chamber is not used, thus becoming valuable fertilizer (which would be too expensive for the farmer to purchase). As it returns to the soil, the cycle of bringing life from death is completed.

Animals are also an important part of a healthy rural ecosystem. Through their manure they return fertility to the soil. If grazed properly, cattle can dramatically improve the health of pasturelands. One study in Zimbabwe found that by using Holistic Management, land could support seven times as many cattle as previously thought possible, even as the health of the pasture increased. As dried-up streams began flowing again, the landowners had to borrow additional cattle to keep the grass down.[12]

Animals may also function as a savings account for the rural family—something that can quickly be turned to cash in an emergency. In addition to providing assistance in veterinary care, Plant With Purpose has borrowed from the Heifer Project model, which gives an animal to a family with the requirement that the first offspring be returned to the organization to be passed on to another family in a pay-it-forward system.

Miracle Trees

When it comes to restoring the environment, helping the poor, or most any other difficult task, there is a temptation to seek a miracle cure. We're inclined to seek the simple, one-size-fits-all solution to all of our problems.

I am frequently asked if we are planting "that miracle tree." But the identity of the miracle tree has changed several times since

Plant With Purpose began. At first, leucaena, a fast-growing tree from Southeast Asia, was the miracle tree. Today it is the moringa. Neem and acacia have each had their turn as the tree that will save the world. Even the oft-disdained eucalyptus was once believed to be the miracle tree that would fix all our problems.

The phenomenon isn't restricted to trees. Jatropha, a plant that produces oil suitable for biodiesel, is being hailed in many places as the cure for the problem of sustainable energy. We have done something similar with corn in the United States.

But creation is far more complicated and subtle. God loves diversity. He gave us many remarkable plants and trees, most of which we are just beginning to appreciate.

CHAPTER 5

Creating Enterprise

A short man with a fedora and worn blazer came toward me with an intense, angry expression. He banged the edge of a coin on the table in front of me, demanding a fine for my improper behavior in the meeting. I paid my shillings, and he moved on to the next violator.

Two groups of thirty members each were attending a fundraiser for our local partner, Floresta Tanzania's savings-led community banks, along with about twenty invited guests, including the Floresta staff. The morning began with introductions, songs, and encouragement. Then every member had the opportunity to contribute to his or her savings account. Each person ceremoniously walked forward and presented his or her shillings to the group officers, who announced to the gathering how much was being deposited before putting it into a big metal box with three padlocks.

Next, vegetables from the members' gardens were auctioned, with the proceeds contributed to the fund. As group members sang, *"Harambe! Harambe!"* (which means "cooperation" or "pulling together as one"), everyone present, including guests, was invited to bring contributions forward. Many danced as they came, waving worn bank notes over their heads.

Throughout the meeting, minor infractions in protocol elicited fines. Guests were usually exempt. However, when our Tanzanian director, Edith Banzi, answered her cell phone in the middle of the collection of shares, the intense man banged his coin at her. I had to laugh. Before I knew it, he was heading toward me.

Overcoming Barriers

Empowerment can take a community a long way. Agricultural skills and technical training can take them even further. But there are often barriers that must be overcome to implement the next steps. A farmer may have agroforestry training but can't afford some specialized inputs. Perhaps a family is paying exorbitant rent or share-cropping the land they farm. They may have an idea for a business but can't afford the materials or inventory needed to start. Or, like the Haitian who was forced to cut his mango trees, they may be so consumed with short-term survival they can't take a longer view. People will stay on their farms and reforest the land only if it makes sense economically. For lasting change, environmental and economic incentives must line up. To accomplish that goal, Plant With Purpose has experimented with various lending systems.

In casual conversation I have heard the terms *microcredit, microfinance,* and *microenterprise* used interchangeably to describe anything from a personal loan made to a local pastor, to a business set up and run by an American hoping to provide jobs in a developing country, to commercial banking services. More precisely, however, *microfinance* refers to a broad array of small financial services including credit, savings, and insurance. *Microcredit* refers to small loans. *Microenterprise* refers to small businesses that may or may not be recipients of microcredit.

Microcredit and microfinance have recently gained enormous visibility. Mohammed Yunus's receipt of the Nobel Peace Prize and the success of Kiva[1] (whose Web site allows people to see those to whom they are lending) have played a role, as have the endorsements of a number of A-list celebrities. This approach appeals to many Americans who are frustrated with charitable giving and prefer a market-based approach.

Plant With Purpose turned to microcredit out of a desire to avoid the dependency created by handouts and subsidies. There is an inverse relationship between subsidy and sustainability. The greater the subsidy, the less sustainable a project or process of change will be when the outside agent (whether it's a church, an NGO, or Plant With Purpose) halts the subsidy and natural economic forces take over.

For example, if I give away food (maximum subsidy), hungry people will be fed, but only until I stop. If I help start a bakery by paying for the flour and firewood (intermediate subsidy), it will probably go out of business when I stop donating. However, if I teach people how to start their own bakery (subsidizing only the training), bearing their own costs, the business survives long after I am gone. (Better still if I find someone who has the drive and interest to start a chicken farm, abandon my idea for a bakery, and instead empower him to pursue his own idea.)

Yet it is difficult to eliminate all subsidies and still catalyze change. Some subsidy is usually necessary, even if it is just the cost of training. To achieve maximum impact, there must be enough of a subsidy to start the process, but it should be kept to a minimum. The optimal amount of subsidy varies depending on the local culture, economic conditions, and a host of other factors. In any case, microcredit is one method for minimizing subsidy and still catalyzing change.

Exercising Caution

Churches with an interest in poverty reduction may want to set up and implement their own microcredit programs. But there are many ways in which a poorly designed microcredit or microenterprise program can go wrong. Not many of us would start a bank as amateurs, but that is what we are attempting when we begin a microcredit operation.

One key to success is the willingness and ability to enforce the collection of loans. If an organization begins to forgive loans, or becomes lax in collection, the loan program will quickly fail. However, creditor-debtor relationships can be a hindrance to ministry. One rarely has a warm fuzzy feeling for his or her creditors.

In Tanzania, before we were able to develop a loan system that was community-owned and -enforced, people would hide when our local director would visit to offer help or see how vegetable gardens were progressing. People assumed Edith was there to collect on loans. That is hardly the relationship most ministries hope to establish.

Other types of income-generation schemes pose dangers as well. The history of attempts to help the poor is rife with stories of well-intended failure. Nonprofit organizations and church volunteers tend to focus on production first and demand second, unlike more business-minded people who look for opportunities in the market. There are numerous stories of products being created with no market.

Many income-generation schemes implemented by outsiders have hidden expenses, so they cost more than they earn. I once evaluated a chicken project in which a large coop had been set up with a heater that cost far more to run than the potential income from the eggs. No one had done the math. Ultimately, projects like this drain confidence from the community members.

Appropriate Credit

Since its founding in 1985, Plant With Purpose has been involved in credit systems and business creation. We have made thousands of loans, ranging from $50 to $5,000. These loans have been used for agroforestry and agricultural inputs as well as a variety of small businesses, including mechanic shops, carpenter's shops, bakeries, beauty salons, and tailors. As a small institution that has been offering credit for many years, we have learned several lessons—some of them the hard way.

Our first initiative was to start a large for-profit tree nursery in the Dominican Republic. Los Arbolitos would be providing high-quality tree seedlings for reforestation, as well as jobs for Dominicans. It was owned by Plant With Purpose in United States, Floresta in the Dominican Republic, and a number of private shareholders.

Its profits would be used to fund Plant With Purpose's other work. Since there were no local sources of tree seedlings, this made sense as an early initiative.

At one time Los Arbolitos was the largest tree nursery in the Caribbean, employing as many as a hundred people, with the capacity to produce up to ten million seedlings annually. However, even though there was much need for reforestation, there was little commercial demand for tree seedlings. The government was our most important client, though it proved to be a fickle one.

Still, Los Arbolitos had several notable achievements. Together with Floresta Dominican Republic, the tree nursery helped increase awareness of deforestation and became part of a growing environmental movement in the Dominican Republic. In his book *Collapse*, Jared Diamond acknowledged this movement as one key reason the Dominican Republic has fared better than Haiti environmentally.[2]

Los Arbolitos also introduced important technologies for producing high-quality tree seedlings. As the government became more aware of the need to reforest, it developed tree nurseries of its own with techniques learned from Los Arbolitos. However, government policy has been to give free tree seedlings to anyone who would plant them, making it virtually impossible for Los Arbolitos to remain profitable.

Los Arbolitos survives today, nearly twenty-five years later, by focusing on the growing demand for ornamental plants. Additionally, the nursery still responds to the occasional large order for tree seedlings. On my last visit, they were processing a government order for nearly two million pine seedlings.

Next we began to make loans specifically for agroforestry. As Roland Bunch points out his classic book, *Two Ears of Corn*, trees are a difficult starting point for agricultural or community development because it takes so long for the farmer to realize any financial or ecological benefit.[3] Most people will not make such a long-term investment unless they can afford to divert current energy and income to it in the hope of someday reaping rewards.

Poor people worry about where their next meal is coming from. A few months between planting and harvesting is a long time when you are hungry. Even the fastest-growing trees provide no income for several years. Plant With Purpose's agroforestry loans, combined with income from short-term crops such as oregano, were designed to give farmers the ability to wait until tree crops could be sold. The principal on these loans was to be paid back when the first tree harvest took place.

Originally, eighty farmers enrolled in this program. With assistance from the InterAmerican Development Bank, we were able to offer loans to another two hundred farmers. This system helped many families become prosperous. But it suffered from several design flaws.

For one thing, it was extremely expensive in terms of cost-per-beneficiary. And it kept capital tied up for a long time, limiting the number of beneficiaries. Although farmers made interest payments using income from the short-term crops, no payments were made on the principal until the trees were harvested, seven to ten years after the loan was made. Many borrowers began to think of it as a grant. In addition, poor farmers with an income of as little as $350 a year often lost all perspective when they received a loan in the amount of $3,000.

In order to ensure repayment, Floresta Dominican Republic controlled the marketing. Farmers sold their wood through Floresta, which subtracted loan payments from the proceeds. Eventually, Floresta became a bottleneck, unable to sell wood while interest accrued to the farmer. In time, many farmers lost a sense of ownership.

From this experience we learned a number of things: We had to start smaller in our financing, require regular payments, set up systems of peer accountability, and provide more freedom for loan recipients to develop their own business plans.

Starting smaller reduces the overall risk for both the lender and the borrower. It also gives the recipients the opportunity to be faithful with a little before they are given much. Most of the people we loan to have no collateral, credit history, or experience. Starting small lets everybody try it out first.

One key incentive for repaying loans on time is the potential to qualify for a larger loan in the future.[4] Smaller loans permit shorter repayment periods, which keeps the promise of a future loan more immediate. This has proven to be one of the most important motivators for the repayment of loans.

Studies have demonstrated the importance of requiring regular small payments in a microcredit system.[5] We didn't require this in our early loans, reasoning that the borrowers would only be able to pay when harvests were sold.

A common misperception with regard to microcredit is that borrowers can only pay off loans with the income generated from the activity financed by the loan.[6] That is, if the loan goes for trees, the borrower will only be able to pay off the loan by selling wood of forest products. However, poor farmers usually have multiple sources of income. Thus, for example, payments could be made on the tree loan with income from the farm or from selling chickens. However, with loans as disproportionately large as Floresta was making for agroforestry, regular payments would have been very difficult.

Freedom for the borrower allows entrepreneurial creativity. It also ensures that the borrower actually wants to engage in the business for which the loan is being made, rather than accessing the capital and diverting it for another use. Even when loans are extended in kind, such as with seeds or equipment, the materials can be accepted and then sold for cash. Giving borrowers the opportunity to decide how they will use their loans helps minimize this temptation.

When we expanded our work into Mexico, we applied the lessons we learned in the Dominican Republic.

For cultural reasons, communities were more willing to establish community tree nurseries or to support reforestation. However, part of our rationale for including a loan program came from realizing how dependent the economies in these communities were on charcoal and firewood. Almost any other small business would be more forest-friendly. So we offered training in business planning, accounting, and marketing, and we formed small-loan groups. I was amazed by the variety of business ideas and the entrepreneurial spirit of the people. Although many of them needed training in business principles, they had a far better sense of what was possible and where their passions lay than we did. Financed businesses include carpentry shops, welding shops, a public phone (the only one in town), restaurants, stores, handicraft manufacturing, various resale activities, and a health clinic. We also funded some agricultural projects, such as small-scale irrigation.

In Haiti the model was again modified. Haitians had less land available, so they could not devote it to woodlots. They didn't need money for tree seedlings because several agencies in the area were giving away seedlings. What they did need was instruction, incentive to plant, and a reason to invest in their land. Thus, rather than making loans directly for agroforestry and tree planting as we had in the Dominican Republic, we made a broader array of loans—but tree planting and implementing sustainable agriculture and agroforestry on one's farm were a prerequisite for receiving credit. Credit brought people into the program, but empowerment and sustainable agriculture training kept them there as its value became evident.

To avoid some of the pitfalls we had in the Dominican Republic, we established peer accountability groups or credit co-ops. Groups of twenty to one hundred people met, received training, established their own constitutions and bylaws, elected officers, and started saving.

When groups demonstrated the ability to save and make loans out of their savings, Floresta Haiti contributed capital to the groups for additional loans. From the farmers' perspective, tree planting and soil conservation become part of the transaction cost of the loan. This cost ultimately benefits the borrower by increasing the health and productivity of their land. It also benefits all those downstream, making it a positive externality worthy of subsidization.

Sustainability

In the world of microfinance and microcredit, one of the most intense debates centers on institutional sustainability. One side of the argument contends that if a micro-lending institution is financially sustainable—that is, if its services pay for themselves—it can dramatically scale up, eliminating reliance on donations and eventually accessing commercial capital. At that point it can reach many times more clients than a subsidized institution, serving many more poor people and making a larger impact on poverty.

On the other side is the idea that once sustainability or even profitability becomes a goal, serving the poor becomes secondary. It is more cost effective to make one loan of $1,000 than to make ten $100 loans, so the organization becomes tempted to give priority to larger clients. Additionally an institution seeking its own profitability will focus on the lowest-cost clients, such as those in easy-to-reach locations, bypassing the remote, rural poor.

To become sustainable, an institution must streamline its operations, or at least separate banking and whatever social services it provides. Agriculture, with its volatility, and forestry, with its delayed benefits, make poor choices for loans if your intent is to be financially sustainable.

In recent years the argument for sustainability has gained the upper hand and microfinance has become more the domain of commercial banks. Many nonprofits are transforming themselves into commercial banks or moving away from offering microfinance services.

Plant With Purpose has no plans to become a bank, and neither should most churches. We see credit as one small, albeit necessary, tool to achieve our integrated outcome. This has led us to seek other models more suited to our limitations.

Savings-Led Credit Systems

When we began work in Tanzania in 2003, we had limited success with credit. However, Edith experimented with a system called VICOBA, which was being tried elsewhere in Tanzania, initiating a trial with the farmers around the base of Mount Kilimanjaro.

VICOBA (Village Community Bank) is a community-based savings-and-loan system developed by CARE in West Africa[7] that is now used in many parts of sub-Saharan Africa. It is based entirely on the savings of the group members, with no outside capital. Each VICOBA group consists of thirty members from the same community who receive three months of intensive training in savings, loans, and business planning. During that time they establish their own norms, draft bylaws, and elect leaders. At each weekly meeting, members make small deposits, purchasing between one and three shares in the group. Every member must purchase at least one share every week and no more than three. The size of the share is agreed upon by the group and may start at about one U.S. dollar. This money becomes the capital from which loans are made.

Interest-bearing loans made to group members help the capital grow. Loans are drawn from the group savings fund and are usually short term (less than six months). Interest rates are set by the group and are locally competitive. Three to four percent per month is typical. That may seem high, but the members are in effect paying interest to themselves. If all the money was loaned out and working all year, with 100 percent efficiency, it could grow by as much as 50 percent per year. In practice the system is less efficient, but savers are still able to earn a healthy rate of return on their investments, while providing loan capital to borrowers.

Another way these groups increase their capital is through the collection of very small fines from members who violate protocol. Arriving late to a meeting is penalized by a fine. Missing a meeting results in a fine, as does talking during a meeting, allowing your cell phone to ring, using the wrong terminology (deposits may be referred to as "bunches of bananas" or "goats" rather than shillings), and a number of other offenses. These fines are collected by a designated fines officer and added to the group savings fund.

In addition to increasing capital, these fines have had a dramatic impact on the local culture. Visiting Tanzanian officials have commented on the unusual punctuality of the people who come to group meetings, or who excuse themselves from other activities to attend their VICOBA meeting. (The fine system has proven so effective that we have incorporated it into our own office procedures in San Diego.)

In addition to the savings fund, VICOBA groups may establish their own charitable funds to assist members with various needs such as medical expenses or other emergencies. Voluntary collections are taken by the group every week, above and beyond shares invested.

Transparency is a key element of the system. Each member is expected to attend every meeting. All members announce how many shares they are investing, and the group acknowledges each member's investment.

Loans are treated similarly. When a loan is made, the funds are given to the individual at the weekly meeting, and the amount is counted in front of the entire group. The savings fund is stored in a heavy metal box with three locks. Three members of the group are selected to hold the keys, and all must be present to open the box. After the box is opened in the presence of all the members, the cash inside is counted and announced to all present. At the end of the meeting, the cash is recounted just before the box is closed and relocked.

The investment cycle is short: in most cases, twelve months. Once the cycle ends, each member's shares plus interest are distributed in a time-bound system, but they may be reinvested into the next cycle.

The primary drawback to a savings-led scheme is that it takes more time to accumulate significant amounts of capital, since it is all generated from within. Nonetheless, it accumulates more rapidly than might be expected.

There are other advantages over the more familiar credit-led models. All infrastructure is built within the community and strengthens the community rather than the NGO or microfinance institution. Many duties that would be managed by loan officers and microfinance employees are handled by volunteers within the community. Thus costs are dramatically reduced, and the structure is sustained by the community itself, independent of the NGO. Our only cost is training.

Additionally, savings opportunities may be more useful to the poor and in greater demand than credit. Contrary to popular belief, the poor are very interested in saving and often willing to pay for the opportunity to deposit their savings, in effect earning negative interest.[8] Some studies have shown that in poor communities there is nearly a five-to-one ratio of savers to borrowers.[9]

Finally, the VICOBAs are a perfect platform for training and have been an active force in encouraging community and group problem solving.

Small loans have been instrumental in changing the economic future for hundreds of farmers. Microcredit has the potential to pay for itself, allowing funds to expand in ways that most non-profit interventions never could. However, credit is not the right tool in every situation. Microcredit has sometimes been regarded as a miracle cure. But loans are just a small part of what it takes to eliminate poverty. Like agroforestry, it sometimes gets overemphasized, and if improperly applied, it has the potential to hurt the poor, creating indebtedness and ill will.

The Most Elegant Solution

Sometimes the tools for creating enterprise already exist in a community and require no loans. This is always the best place to start.

For example, in Oaxaca, the abundant pine trees had been utilized primarily for illegal firewood and lumber. Lumber was often cut using chainsaws, wasting much of the wood.

Misión Integral, our Mexican partner, found a local teacher to show the women in the community how to make baskets from the long pine needles and sell them at market. Many of the women had never brought anything to market before, and they expressed nervousness about setting up a market stall. To their delight and surprise, the baskets sold. The first baskets were crude, but when groups of women in other communities also started making them, competition grew and both quality and variety greatly improved.

As the women began to contribute to the family income, their self-esteem improved. One woman told us that Mixtec women are traditionally seen as good only for making tortillas and babies, but now her husband treated her with respect.

Additionally, pine trees now have a more immediate and sustainable use besides firewood. There is now an incentive to plant trees. If someone plants a pine for the wood, he will not receive an economic benefit for twenty-five years or longer. However, even a small, young tree can produce pine needles.

In an effort to ensure the sustainability of the project, we verified that there was a local market for these baskets. It was not our desire for the communities to become dependent on us to sell their products for their ongoing support, creating an artificial market.

The purpose of helping create enterprise is to give communities the tools they need to prosper and to live in harmony with their Creator and his creation long after we are gone. This project takes advantage of resources that already exist in the community and markets that are accessible by the community. People are able to benefit economically from the sustainable use of the forest and have an incentive to care for it. It is one small project, but a perfect example of the type of virtuous cycle that is possible.

CHAPTER 6

Sharing the Gospel

As we sat in chilly darkness of the Dominican field office, the woman's wailing filled the night. We had arrived in the village of Sabana Real a few minutes ago, having made the long, steep drive into the mountains that straddle the border between Haiti and the Dominican Republic.

"*Ay, Dios mio! Dios mio!*" Getting out of the trucks, we learned from whispered explanations that the eleven-year-old son of a Dominican farmer was missing. Residents believed the young boy had been kidnapped by a sixteen-year-old Haitian field worker who was also missing. As we sat in the office and prayed, we heard the angry voices of a mob that had gathered a few hundred feet up the road. A group of Haitians were being held in a home nearby, threatened with violence, until soldiers from the nearby military guard post intervened.

Quirico, a pastor who works with Plant With Purpose and the grandfather of the missing eleven-year-old, did his best to encourage calm. All night and the next morning, teams of men combed the hillsides or hurried off to track down the latest rumor.

Throughout the following day the boy remained missing. Then a villager contacted a *houngan,* or Vodou priest, in San Cristobal.

He told the searchers to look for the little boy's body just down the hill from our office, which is where the body was found.

The sixteen-year-old was soon apprehended and charged with murder. He'd been hired by a neighbor across the border in Haiti after a quarrel that began with a sheep grazing in someone's garden. Nine months later the older boy's mother was murdered, probably in retaliation. Meanwhile, the eerie prescience of the *houngan* helped the traditional Haitian religion of Vodou gain credibility in Sabana Real.

People sometimes ask me why we feel the need to have a spiritual impact in our work. My experience in Sabana Real is all the reminder I need that, without God, all the development and environmental restoration in the world will not bring transformation.

Haiti and the Dominican Republic share the same island but could not be more different culturally. Haiti is much poorer, and the environmental difference between the two countries is well publicized. The dynamic on the border is analogous to that of the U.S./Mexican border. Some estimates place as many as a million Haitians living and working illegally in the Dominican Republic.[1] The Dominican economy is dependent on Haitian labor, yet most Dominicans resent the presence of the Haitians in their country. Prejudice, both racial and cultural, runs deep and goes all the way back to the days when Haiti invaded the Dominican Republic in the early nineteenth century. Relations reached their nadir in the 1930s when Rafael Trujillo, dictator of the Dominican Republic, ordered the Dominican military to murder nearly thirty thousand Haitians and Dominicans of Haitian ancestry who were living along the border. Fearing a Haitian invasion, Trujillo planted a number of Dominican villages, including Sabana Real in the remote and mountainous border areas of Independencia.

Today, the Haitian side of the border is densely populated, and availability of farmland is limited. The Dominicans, on the other hand, have land in abundance, though much of it steep, forested, and ill-suited to agriculture. However, with plentiful Haitian labor, it is a simple matter to farm beans on any available land, leading to rapid deforestation and dramatic erosion. Some Haitians live in small shacks on the Dominican farms, while others walk for hours, crossing the border daily to work for wages or in exchange for a portion of their crop. In the Floresta office, before the murder, we often heard them at four in the morning, walking to hillside fields miles inside the Dominican Republic.

In an effort to model Christ's kingdom, Floresta Haiti and Floresta Dominican Republic established a joint project to work on both sides of the border. We are well aware that the economic and environmental fault lines separating the countries are dramatic. A spiritual battle is taking place as well but the boundaries are not as clear cut. Godly and ungodly people can be found on both sides of the border, as good and evil run through all of us.

Of course, damaging beliefs and prejudices are not limited to this area of the globe. Recent news articles have highlighted the plight of Tanzanian albinos, whose body parts are believed to have magical powers, resulting in persecution, murder, and dismemberment.[2]

Plant With Purpose works in an area of Burundi that has experienced years of brutal civil war based on ethnic hatred. There, as in Rwanda, violence between Hutu and Tutsi has devastated the country, leaving it one of the poorest in the world. Jared Diamond has pointed out the environmental dimension to this conflict.[3] Its resolution lies in spiritual transformation. Repentance, forgiveness, and a radical change of heart are necessary.

Ten years ago I visited a tiny island in the Solomons in the South Pacific that was once known for headhunting. Two young men took me to one of the village's "traditional sites." There, in the shadow of a small volcano, in the overgrown jungle, were four or five large piles of rocks. Each pile covered a mound of human skulls. One man pointed to each pile and named its origin. "These are the skulls collected from Ghizo. These are the people from Kolambangara." He paused and smiled. "But that was my grandfather's time. Now we have Jesus." If ever I heard a convincing argument for Christian witness, it was in that smiling statement.

Perhaps no other area of Plant With Purpose's work is more controversial than our efforts in evangelism and discipleship. Some of this arises from projecting American cultural biases onto the people who live where Plant With Purpose works. Secular thought is a foreign thing in many places around the world, where everything has a spiritual component. Bryant Myers points out that Christians are always witnessing, whether for Christ or for some other worldview. If we are silent, we are giving mute assent to the local explanation for how the world works, or alternately we are giving testimony to a worldview in which technology holds the answers.[4]

Another reason sharing the gospel is controversial is the insensitive way in which it is often done. I once picked up a magazine in a guest house in Haiti, published by the denomination that ran the place. It contained an article written by a short-term mission team that implied they had brought Jesus to a place where the gospel had never been heard and single-handedly defeated Satan in the process. In a week they had allegedly changed this part of Haiti completely, probably without ever learning anyone's name! Such attitudes do a tremendous disservice to both the local churches and the work God is already doing in a community. As Bryant Myers says, God has been at work in the story of a community before outsiders get there, and he will be at work in that community long after the outsiders leave.[5]

It is easy to romanticize the poor, their communities, and their traditional beliefs. It is just as easy to demonize a whole culture, people, and way of life. We must avoid either extreme. Rather, we must be confident in the truth and goodness of the gospel we've been given to proclaim while being respectful of both the people and the work God is doing in their midst. As we humbly share the hope Christ has given us, we become more aware of our own cultural and spiritual blind spots. We must remember that we are not the saviors, Jesus is. And spiritual development is a process of mutual discovery and growth in the body of Christ.

Discipleship

At the end of the gospel of Matthew, Jesus gives the Great Commission: to go and make disciples of all nations, teaching them to obey his commandments to love God and love our neighbors (Matthew 28:19-20). This is often interpreted as going and

Creation Care and Worship

Whenever we sing the Doxology in church, we sing out the words, "Praise God from whom all blessings flow. Praise him all creatures here below." Note that *all* creatures are referred to in this hymn. These words have become so familiar to us that we sometimes fail to see the implications of what we are singing.

We humans are not the only ones called upon to worship God. If you read Psalm 148, you will find that King David called upon all living creatures to worship the Almighty. Even more strange to those of us steeped in modernity is that, in this psalm, even that which is inanimate is called upon to worship God.

Almost a thousand years ago, St. Francis of Assisi went out to the fields and called upon the birds to sing hymns of praise to the Lord. He called upon the sheep to raise their voices to make sounds of praise to God. He called upon the cows to do the same. He believed, as the Bible teaches, that all of creation was spoken into existence for the glory of God.

Sometimes our environmentalism is completely utilitarian. We want to save nature because we humans need it for our survival and well-being—and I am not arguing with that reality. Romans 8:19-23 says that God's children are called upon to rescue creation from its present degraded condition.

But there is a deeper reason for saving nature. That deeper reason is that everything that was created was created to worship God. For instance, the heavens were created to declare the glory of God. They weren't created simply for our own personal enjoyment.

Psalm 148:7 reads, "Praise the LORD from the earth, you sea monsters and all deeps." I believe the "sea monsters" who praise God in that verse are whales. Whales sing, and if there were no human beings on this planet, whales would still have a function that is glorious; that function is to sing hymns of praise to God. Anyone who has ever taken time to listen to the songs of whales knows there is a mystical quality to their singing that makes it easy to understand their ultimate purpose is to sing praise to God. If a species of whale is made extinct because of human irresponsibility, it is not just that we've lost an interesting creature from the face of the earth. As tragic as that is, the full reality is even more troubling: We have silenced a special voice of praise to the Almighty.

This is not some new age proposal. Throughout the Bible we sense what one philosopher called "a great chain of being"—with God and the angels at the top, humans below them, animals below us, and then the plant kingdom, and the inorganic realities of nature. The Bible is clear that all of creation was meant to glorify God. And when Adam and Eve fell, creation suffered along with that first couple. In Romans Paul reminds us that it is not just us humans who long to be restored to where we can worship God in fullness and joy. "The whole creation has been groaning in labor pains," waiting to be delivered for exactly the same purpose.

To interfere with worship is blasphemy. Thus, the obliteration of the environment has blasphemous dimensions to it. Considering what we have done to nature, we need to repent, because we have hindered nature's glorification of the God who created all things in heaven and on earth to praise his name.

Tony Campolo is professor emeritus of sociology at Eastern University in St. Davids, Pennsylvania.

making *converts* of all nations. Yet disciples are far more than merely converts. They are imitators of Christ, loving God and actively loving their neighbors.

Prior to the genocide, Rwanda had the highest percentage of Christians in Africa and was considered a missionary success story.[6] Clearly, something was missing. The world is full of people who call themselves Christians. Disciples are harder to find.

At Plant With Purpose we have always emphasized discipleship rather than evangelism. It would be nice to say that emphasis was the result of deep theological reflection and prayer—and there was certainly much of that. But as much as anything, our focus on discipleship owes itself to pure practicality. Eldon Garcia, Floresta's director in the Dominican Republic for many years, told me he saw a pattern with some of the farmers who succeeded in our program. The story wasn't pretty.

As these farmers grew more successful, they suddenly had more money than ever before. And their lives began to change. First came the television, then more alcohol, and finally mistresses. Not exactly the transformation and development we were hoping for. A lot of microfinance organizations deal with this problem by focusing on women, who tend to be more responsible and family-oriented than men. But since we were working with farmers, we didn't have that option.

We became convinced that none of the physical and environmental changes would last if there wasn't also a change of heart and character. We discovered that the root cause of poverty wasn't a lack of material goods, or even deforestation. It was broken relationships. In order to see real development, the fundamental relationships between people and God, people and their neighbors, and people and their land had to change. Unless people's hearts and minds are transformed, much development work goes for naught.

We also began to see the importance of a kingdom focus. The gospel is far more than merely a road map to heaven. Conversion, of course, is a first step, but we are fundamentally interested in transformed lives. James tells us faith without works is dead. But a living faith asks, "What does this good news imply for how I live my life, and how I treat my neighbor and the land God has given me?"

We take seriously Christ's rhetorical question, "What good is it for a man to gain the whole world, yet forfeit his soul?" (Mark 8:36, NIV). It is our desire that everyone we come in contact with, each individual we serve, will come to know Jesus. Thus we go out of our way to make opportunities to learn more about Jesus available to all who wish to pursue them.

In John 6, Jesus reminds his listeners of the manna that was provided to the Israelites in the wilderness. He contrasts himself to the manna: He is the Bread of Life, and those who have him will never be hungry again. As life-giving as the manna was, he is more so. Similarly, he is the Living Water, and those who drink it will never thirst again.

We want to give the poor bread and water. But as life-giving as agricultural produce and clean water are, this is not the best we have to give. It would be a shame if we gave only the manna that is gone after a day, when it is in our power to offer the true bread of Jesus.

By the same token, making disciples is not the principle reason behind the development work we do. Once our efforts become a means to an end, even an end as good as this, they become disingenuous. I do not feed, clothe, and educate my children *so* I can share the gospel with them. I feed them, clothe them, educate them, *and* share the gospel with them because I love them.

The Local Church

Plant With Purpose works in partnership with local Christians, professional agronomists, foresters, development professionals, and pastors. Much like our work in farming or reforestation, in which we do not directly farm and plant trees but empower local communities to do so, when it comes to discipleship, our goal is to collaborate with and empower local churches.

In the predominantly Christian countries in which Plant With Purpose works, churches are among the most important institutions in their communities. However, like the communities (and like our own churches), they often lack awareness of their own power and calling.

For many years we neglected the churches in the Dominican Republic. Church leadership seemed weak or nonexistent. Either the pastors had little or no training, or they commuted from the capital and served multiple congregations. However, the churches were central to what was happening in the villages, and any organization hoping to do development there would need to work with local churches in some way. They could not be ignored if we were to engage the community effectively.

We began talking with the pastors of local churches to determine their needs and priorities. In the Dominican Republic, we discovered a pressing need for training of lay leadership. So, in collaboration with the Dominican Bible League, we offered curriculum and training for lay Bible study leaders. Leaders were taught how to study the Bible and how to facilitate small groups, and then they were asked to form Bible studies.

Working with a network of more than sixty rural churches, we facilitated the establishment of hundreds of weekly Bible studies involving thousands of people. Nominal Christians began discovering what their faith was all about as they learned what Scripture teaches, many for the first time. Additionally, the Bible studies provided a non-threatening way for those outside the church, many of them unbelievers, to learn more about what the Bible teaches. Hundreds of people have come to Christ as a result.

As we work to support and empower local churches, these churches are able to support us in a synergistic way, providing validation of our work. Churches are challenged to make a difference in their communities, either directly supporting Plant With Purpose's work or filling the gaps in areas we don't address, such as caring for orphans or providing education for those who cannot go to public school.

A favorite example of the type of synergy that develops comes from Tanzania. Edith and I took several pastors to a conference on creation care in Kenya. I was one of the presenters, and in the course of my presentation, I showed a slide of the devastated forests around Mt. Kilimanjaro National Park. Pastor Lyamuya approached me later and, with an embarrassed smile, explained how convicting it was to see the photo from his own community. "God entrusted it to us to take care of, and we aren't doing our job."

He returned home determined to make a difference. Collaborating with a number of other pastors in the area, he encouraged all the churches to establish tree nurseries. They required those going through confirmation classes to plant trees as a prerequisite to graduation. As a result of these initiatives, nearly 500,000 trees have been planted.

Pastors in that community have also reported a significant increase in church attendance. The first time I attended church in Tanzania, I was startled to hear a live chicken clucking from behind the pulpit. Then I realized that much of the Sunday morning offering was in the form of produce from gardens and farms, laid at the altar. There was a stigma associated with bringing nothing. Now that bio-intensive gardens were providing vegetables and basic income for even the poorest families, everyone had something to bring.

The virtuous cycle created when we support the local church, and the local church supports us, continues. Working together for the kingdom, we can make a much greater difference in the lives of the members of the community.

Back to the Future

When environmental restoration, economic opportunity and discipleship combine, real transformation can take place. We have seen tastes of that transformation, giving us glimpses of the kingdom.

The residents of El Porvenir, Mexico, the village described in chapter 2, are moving toward a more hopeful future. Having realized their considerable talents, they began a sewing enterprise, a bakery, a fish farm, and numerous agroforestry and vegetable farms. Homes now have composting latrines and fuel-saving stoves with chimneys to protect the families from smoke. Where once the community produced only tortillas and beans, on my last visit they offered me fish tacos with garden vegetables and freshly baked bread. Children are healthier with a diversified diet.

They have also taken it upon themselves to start a community tree nursery and have planted thousands of trees on their once-barren hillsides. Rainwater is harvested from rooftops and stored in cisterns. People who left the area have begun to return. The churches are active in their community, and many of the denominational rivalries have been overcome. Silvio Miguel Lopez, the pastor of the Presbyterian church in nearby Santa Ynez, said:

El Porvenir has changed. It is not like it was when I left. Now I see that there are more trees, people have plants and vegetable gardens around their homes. I also see that they are producing trees in their nursery and that the people are planting vetiver grass on the hillsides. The fish production impressed me. They said to me, "What seemed impossible now is possible." I believe that the community should give much thanks to God and to those who have helped them make this possible.

We have seen transformation in the lives of countless individuals as well. I once sat with the Floresta's Dominican staff in a busy café on the main north-south highway in the Dominican Republic. The noise was so loud we had to shout to make ourselves heard. Over the sounds of traffic, spurious car alarms, nearby conversations, and music, our sawmill manager, Cristian, told me his story.

He'd been working for Floresta for twelve years, starting as the night watchman at our warehouse when he was a teenager. In the late 1980s, when Cristian was just twelve years old, his father had received one of the first farm loans from Floresta. After the first tree seedlings were delivered to his father's farm, he felt excited as he and his brothers helped plant them. They represented hope and opportunity.

The neighbors were skeptical. "You can't eat trees," they said. But Cristian's father proved the skeptics wrong. "Our family made more money on that first harvest than had ever passed through our hands before."

Later, his father worked at the Floresta warehouse during the day, and Cristian got a job as night watchman. He moved into sales, helping farmers sell their oregano and later their wood, before coming to work in the main office about five years ago. During that time he went to college, then returned to Floresta, where he runs the sawmill.

Cristian credits Floresta with changing his life and his father's life. "Floresta made it possible for my siblings and me to stay in school." Later he told me, "You should see the house I grew up in, and you should see where my father lives today." He came back to Floresta to share the blessing he received with others.

Later in the afternoon we paid a visit to the home of Luis Garcia, another of the first Floresta farmers. When I visited him fifteen years ago, his wooden house sat on a barren hilltop in the village of Tocoa, and most of the poor farmers in that region grew cassava. Now he lives in a neat cinderblock home with glass windows and electricity, situated in a pleasant grove of trees surrounded by orchards. The barren hilltop is almost unrecognizable. Most of the children I'd met on previous visits are now college graduates.

The following evening we visited a Bible study group in the town of Los Mogotes. As the study concluded, I was introduced to a young man named Jonathan. He had been attending the study for some time and had committed his life to Christ three months earlier.

As we talked, I discovered he was the grandson of one of the first farmers to receive a loan in that area. Although he grew up farming, he is now preparing to go to college.

These three stories—of Cristian and his father, Luis Garcia and his children, and Jonathan and his grandfather—represent long-term success. The fruit of the harvest has been an enduring testimony to what is possible with God.

One of my favorite passages of Scripture, and one we often draw on in Plant With Purpose, comes from Isaiah 41. The Lord, speaking through the prophet Isaiah, says:

> The poor and needy search for water,
> but there is none;
> their tongues are parched with thirst.
> But I the LORD will answer them. . . .
> I will make rivers flow on barren heights,
> and springs within the valleys. . . .
> I will put in the desert
> the cedar and the acacia, the myrtle and the olive.
> I will set pines in the wasteland,
> the fir and the cypress together,
> so that people may see and know . . .
> that the hand of the LORD has done this.
>
> —*Isaiah 41:17-20* (NIV)

The initial problem in this passage is that the poor are suffering from lack of water. God answers them by planting trees and causing springs to flow in the wilderness. The purpose of all that—the needs of the poor being met, trees planted, water flowing—is to glorify God. We hope to play a part in bringing about this prophecy as we work to bring healing, redemption, and good news to places where poverty and environmental degradation intersect.

Environmental restoration leading to economic opportunity is a virtuous cycle. As it brings glory to God, it becomes a victorious cycle, a foreshadowing of the kingdom to come.

CHAPTER 7

The Global View

In the summer of 1996, Nancy and I went to Lake Louise in Alberta, Canada, for our honeymoon. I'd worked right up to the day of the wedding, and I was weary from spending so much time focused on the degraded corners of the earth. I was ready to forget the torn, diminished shadow of former glory that we were confronting on the hillsides of Haiti and the Dominican Republic. Surely if there was a refuge, it would be in the Canadian Rockies. I was looking forward to recharging in the crisp, pristine wilderness of the north.

It didn't take long to discover that this gorgeous country, with its calendar-art landscapes, was under threat too. It wasn't as obvious or as ugly as in the hills of Haiti, but the challenges were quite apparent to those who knew what to look for.

On our trip I asked a few questions and learned of the imbalances threatening the wildlife in Alberta. Invasive species were eliminating most of the native fish. Forests were unhealthy as a result of fire suppression. Habitat was fragmented and rapidly diminishing. Logging and mining were encroaching. Many animals were on the verge of extinction.[1]

It was a startling turning point in my life. If *this* place is endangered, what corner of the earth was untrammeled? I have been on a quest for that spot ever since. My conclusion is that it no longer exists. There is no healthy place left.

In 1999 Nancy and I spent almost six months backpacking around the world. We visited a number of missions and development programs with an eye to improving our work with Plant With Purpose. But I was also trying to get as far off the beaten track as time would allow, looking for the unspoiled spot.

We visited the Solomon Islands, a small archipelago east of Papua New Guinea. One reason I love the Solomon Islands is that it is off the radar, with only a few thousand visitors every year. But being out of the way hasn't helped it environmentally. Rather, its invisibility allows injustice to be perpetrated without the rest of the world taking notice. Upon arrival, we found foreign logging companies stripping the islands, taking advantage of decentralized traditional land-ownership laws.

In New Zealand we got a firsthand lesson on how destructive invasive species can be to native populations. There are more exotic plant species in New Zealand than native ones,[2] and much of the native wildlife is endangered. Exotic possums, deer, rodents, and other mammals have had a devastating effect on vegetation and birds. Tremendous effort has been put into trying to control them and mitigate the damage they have wrought.[3]

Later in the trip we visited Taman Negara, an enormous national park in the rainforest of mainland Malaysia where elephants, tigers, and rhinos still roam. After a long bus ride, we caught a boat for a three-hour trip up the Sungai Tembeling. In long wooden canoes, with just a foot of freeboard and water seeping between the planks as we worked through the rapids, we were treated to the rainforest as we had always imagined it. Lianas hung over the river, the canopy was full of pink and yellow flowers, and flashes of bright color and movement indicated the presence of hornbills and other birds. Unfortunately, the color was just as often an old juice carton; the movement, bits of plastic bag caught in a tree.

Later we visited Nepal and hiked a portion of the Annapurna Circuit. When we arrived, Kathmandu's sanitation workers were striking, garbage filled the streets, and the foul air quality was shocking. In the choking black smoke of the city, many pedestrians wore masks. As we took the plane to see Mount Everest, we had to climb thousands of feet before we cleared the smog to where we could begin to see the peaks sticking up like islands in a vast sea of brown.

Hiking around Annapurna we learned of the deforestation caused by woodstoves and the deadly landslides that followed. We also found out about sanitation issues and saw the vast amounts of litter (especially plastic water bottles) that had been carried into the mountains and then dumped in the canyons. Everywhere we looked, nature was in retreat.

Africa is no different. Flying from Nairobi to Lake Victoria over the Rift Valley in a small plane, I saw no space that was unsettled, no land that was uncultivated. Tin roofs glinted in the sunlight from horizon to horizon. Lake Victoria has been badly damaged by deforestation, contamination, and the introduction of invasive species. Water hyacinth is choking out other life, while introduced Nile perch have eliminated most native species of fish. A group of friends who visited a month earlier all contracted schistosomiasis after swimming in the water.

A high-end resort on Rusinga Island in Lake Victoria manages to maintain the image of pristine beauty in the midst of remote wilderness. I was reminded of the concept of "landscape amnesia" that Jared Diamond introduces in *Collapse*.[4] This has also been called the "shifting baseline syndrome."[5] Like the frog in a pot of water who doesn't notice when the water is gradually heated to the boiling point, environmental changes happen so slowly that we do not recognize as they occur. We forget what things looked like originally. We can only guess what Lake Victoria must have been like 150 years ago when John Speke first laid eyes on it. Since we are unable to compare its current state with its previous state, we fail to see the degradation. However, the lake has become a shadow of its former self.

I have witnessed this effect in Southern California, where the canyons and mesas of my home have been gradually reduced to a few thin slivers of park in the midst of housing developments. Most of the people who live here are recent arrivals and have no

Climate Change

I watched her thin hands as she clutched a small handmade shovel, scratching the hard surface of the soil. The energy needed to make a dent in the soil far surpassed the strength of this AIDS widow and mother of four young children.

That hot day in Zambia carried several messages. The seasons are now unpredictable. The rains barely came during the last rainy season, which brought on an early drought. As a result, this caring mother was still trying to plant a garden in some borrowed space in hopes there would be food for the next season. Her strength waned in the hot sun as her frail body, weakened by hunger, had little endurance. Yet she had no food or water for her family for that day, which meant she had several hours of searching and walking to find food to feed her family.

I wish I could say this particular season was an anomaly, but climate change is real. People who have lived with the soil for generations are mystified. One village elder said, "Things are strange. We have been able to predict the beginning and end of the rains and the exact days to plant, but now we are confused."

Working in relief and development calls for study in crop adaptation, as well as mitigation on the prevention side. In the meantime, people need to eat and retain dignity in their own self-sufficiency. This is an urgent call to action.

JoAnne Lyon is the founder and chair of the board of directors for World Hope International and general superintendent of The Wesleyan Church.

idea what a beautiful place this once was. What had been here for millennia disappeared in thirty years—and we have barely missed it. Dr. Jeremy Jackson, professor of oceanography at Scripps Institution of Oceanography, writes, "The problem is that everyone, scientists included, believes that the way things were when they first saw them is natural."[6]

When we read Jared Diamond's account of the destruction of the ecosystem of Easter Island and that society's subsequent demise, we may pass judgment on the short-sightedness of the islanders, without recognizing the mirror it provides us. Diamond speculates that the islander who cut down the last tree probably didn't recognize its significance. By that time trees must have long since lost their prominence in the landscape. With many plants and creatures, we are not far from this today.

C. S. Lewis, author of *The Chronicles of Narnia* and *Mere Christianity*, wrote a poem hinting at the same idea, titled "The Future of Forestry." In it he imagines a time in the near future when children will have difficulty imagining what elms, chestnuts, and even autumn looked like during a legendary "age of trees" before concrete covered the land.[7]

It is hard to grasp the big picture unless we are actively studying it, and even then specialization makes it difficult. Most of us have seen only a small part of the world and we have no sense of how it looked before.

However, the picture we've been given by scientific research is no more reassuring than my anecdotal conclusions. Once you begin to connect the dots, the truth is grim. Matthew Sleeth, one of the leaders in the Christian creation-care movement, put it succinctly: "The world is dying."[8] On a bright spring day it can be hard to imagine this is true. But once you open your eyes, it is unmistakable. And unspeakably sad.

Global Issues

Dozens of serious ecological issues confront us today. The list below is by no means comprehensive, but it highlights some of the most troublesome concerns.

• Deforestation

We have already considered several examples of the localized effects of deforestation; however, it is a problem of global significance. Thirteen million hectares are being leveled annually, reducing biodiversity, changing local and global rainfall patterns, contributing to desertification, and impacting climate change.[9] Forests provide dozens of services that are absolutely essential, yet underappreciated, services such as protecting watersheds and directly contributing to the availability and quality of fresh water. Jared Diamond points out that deforestation was among the principal causes for the collapse of all the societies he examined.[10] Furthermore, deforestation is the second-largest source for the release of carbon dioxide into the atmosphere after the burning of fossil fuels.[11]

Even forests that are not being cut are in poor health, and trees are dying in increasing numbers. Weakened by drought, smog, and other environmental issues, as well as by poor forest management, trees have become more vulnerable to pests. In the Pacific Northwest, the rate of tree mortality has doubled in the last seventeen years.[12] Pines in British Columbia, Alberta, California, and elsewhere are dying at a stunning rate.

Nancy and I once spent most of a day driving through startlingly red forests of dead lodge-pole pines in British Columbia. In the wilderness areas near my home, over the last five years we have grown accustomed to mountains without pine trees, as they have been destroyed by bark beetle, fire, and pollution.

• Biodiversity

Many biologists believe we are in the midst of a human-induced mass extinction. Some predict up to half of all species may be extinct within the next hundred years.[13]

Discussions of biodiversity loss often become utilitarian, framed in terms of the potential impact on humans. *Time* magazine raised this question in a recent article: "When we are using the term *extinction* to talk about the fate of the U.S. auto industry, does it really matter if we lose species like the Holdridge's toad, the Yangtze river dolphin, and the golden toad?"[14] Yet the symphony of creation, created to sing praise to the Creator, is being silenced to feed our convenience and consumption habits.

Furthermore there is still so little we know about how these things work together to sustain life on earth. We are like a teenager who rebuilds a car in the garage and, when he has finished, finds several pieces left over. He has no idea where they fit or whether the car will run without them, yet he cavalierly tosses them aside. We are throwing away pieces without fully understanding their function.

• Land Degradation

A recent study determined that fifteen out of twenty-four vital ecosystem services that humans rely on for survival are being degraded or used unsustainably on a global level. Declining services include fisheries, genetic resources, fresh water, water purification, erosion regulation, air quality, pollination, and others. Our ability to produce food continues to increase, but as climate, desertification, soil erosion, and water become larger issues, that will likely change.[15]

Soil loss and the widespread loss of arable land are major issues that challenge our future ability to feed ourselves. In many places the only thing that keeps agriculture productive is the continuous addition of fossil-fuel-dependent chemical fertilizers. This has profound implications for humankind.

In the Sahel region of Africa, desertification has led to famine and starvation for those dependent on the land. Once again, it is part of a vicious cycle, as the impact of human practices of overgrazing, deforestation, and ground-water use have contributed to the desertification of once productive land.[16] With the desert come new pests, new diseases, and hunger. But this phenomenon is not limited to Africa. Desertification impacts large areas of China, Central Asia, the United States, South America, and Australia. According to the United Nations, desertification and land degradation threaten as much as a third of the earth's surface and one billion people.[17]

• Oceans and Water

The health of the oceans is in a steep decline. Because of overfishing, agricultural runoff, pollution, and acidification, they are rapidly dying.

The Death of a Way of Life

Thirty years ago, as a young scholar, I conducted fieldwork among the Gabra pastoralists of the Kenya-Ethiopian frontier, where I spent a considerable amount of time learning their culture, language, and history. I wanted to learn how they have been able to survive and flourish in one of Africa's harshest and—from most outside perspectives—most inhospitable environments.

As the Gabra elders, both men and women, taught me their traditions, knowledge, and wisdom, I learned that shepherding their camels, sheep, goats, and cattle over vast, largely waterless, and extremely dry rangelands required an intimate knowledge of vegetation types and locations, as well as wildlife ecology. Those herd owners whose environmental and historical knowledge was deepest and most comprehensive consistently owned the largest herds of animals, and were extensively sought out for advice and counsel. Those herd owners whose knowledge was less extensive regularly struggled and were most vulnerable in the face of recurrent environmental and management challenges.

For the Gabra, the challenges and opportunities of resource variability and climatic change demand proactively positioning human and livestock populations to take advantage of water and rangeland resources wherever and whenever they are located. To do this, the Gabra have learned to count, remember, and predict. They count times of the day, the number of days in seasons and parts of seasons within the solar year, the days in a solar year,

Many of the first Europeans to come to the Americas were cod fisherman, who described fish so abundant as to be almost unbelievable. Today cod fisheries are virtually gone.[18] Some scientists believe that more than 90 percent of large fish such as tuna, swordfish, and sharks are gone.[19] Twenty-nine percent of major commercial fisheries have collapsed, providing less than 10 per-

climate, and events that cycle according to different criteria. They remember patterns from the past. They predict based on events and cycles they have perceived. For the Gabra, survival is counting, remembering numbers and cycles, and predicting, anticipating, and responding proactively. To survive and flourish, they must be right.

For the past three decades, I have observed how the Gabra survive seasons of abundance and scarcity, periods of devastating drought and plentiful rain. I have followed their responses to variations in timing, location, and intensity of these periods. Their understandings and responses have consistently been validated. Those elders who understand the environmental signals and who, because of their knowledge, position their camps and livestock to take advantage of bounty or to mitigate insufficiency, continue to succeed and help others succeed. Those elders without this knowledge have lost livestock, become impoverished, moved to famine camps, and become dependent on relief.

The last time I visited the Gabra, at the turn of this millennium, I met Yatani Sorale, who became my guide, teacher, and mentor. The Gabra consider him the sage and prophet of this generation of elders. He said to me, "We no longer see the patterns. They are no more. We are finished. We have reached the end of counting." Yatani Sorale sat among his peers, his mind increasingly clouded and confused by frameworks that no longer made sense. He died six months later.

A way of life is dying as well.

Dr. Paul Robinson is professor and director of the Human Needs & Global Resources Program at Wheaton College.

cent of their original yield.[20] The absolute catch leveled off and began declining in the late 1980s, at same time the average depth at which fish were being caught significantly increased. Even as the search expanded, the numbers shrank.

A recent study compared photographs of "trophy" fish caught in the reefs of the Florida Keys.[21] In fifty years, average sizes had declined from forty-four pounds and six and half feet to five pounds and one foot. Some experts predict seafood will cease to exist in another fifty years.[22]

Thus far we have largely ignored this trend simply by paying more and eating different kinds of fish. If you go to a seafood restaurant today, you will no longer see on the menu many of the things people ate just twenty years ago. Much of what we eat now was not commercially fished until the more desirable fish became scarce.

If you ever need a reminder of God's endless creativity and love for diversity, there is no place like a coral reef. The Solomon Islands features 485 species of coral and nearly a thousand species of fish, making it one of the most beautiful and incredibly diverse ecosystems in existence.[23] Yet around the world, coral reefs are dying, with 20 percent already gone.[24]

Major portions of the ocean are becoming completely lifeless. Agricultural runoff has led to algae blooms, which have depleted the oxygen to the point where fish can no longer live. Elevated carbon dioxide in the atmosphere is leading to the acidification of the water. To add insult to injury, the existance of an enormous soup of plastic garbage in the midst of the North Pacific Ocean, estimated to contain one hundred million tons of plastic in an area twice the size of Texas, has recently been publicized.[25]

But it is not just the oceans we are poisoning. Matthew Sleeth points out that as many as seven hundred human-made toxins can now be found in human tissue.[26] In his former work as an emergency-room physician, he saw a tremendous increase in cancer, asthma, and other environmentally related ailments. His concern that we were slowly poisoning both ourselves and the world around us led Sleeth to leave that job and become an evangelist for creation care.

Waterborne illness is another form of poisoning and one of the biggest killers in the world today. More than one billion people lack access to clean water, and more than five thousand people die every day from this situation, most of them children.[27] Matters will only get worse as population growth, deforestation, and climate change impact both supply and demand.

• Climate Change

This issue tends to be most controversial because it carries with it profound policy and lifestyle implications. Despite many years working in creation care, I had, until recently, been only marginally aware of the implications of climate change. Deforestation kept me focused, and I rationalized that, whether climate change was real or not, it wouldn't change what we were doing. We would still help the rural poor to fight deforestation and poverty.

However, a little research points out the fallacy of this approach. Climate change is already having a huge impact on people around the world, and the poor feel that impact disproportionately. My Hezekiah attitude ("At least it won't happen in my lifetime") was not only selfish; it was misplaced.

We've already seen some early symptoms of climate change in North America: drought in the Southeast, dying forests in Canada and Alaska, fires in California. Many experts believe the severity of Hurricane Katrina can be attributed to climate change. As a San Diegan, I witnessed the massive evacuation that took place during the firestorms of 2007. Nearly one million people were moved from their homes over the course of the week, at least 1,500 homes were lost, and nine people died in the fires. But those fires occurred in an area of relative wealth and in a country with tremendous resources and the ability to adapt. For most of us, the fires were simply an inconvenience. A similar scenario happening in Port-au-Prince, for example, is horrifying to imagine.

The Intergovernmental Panel on Climate Change (IPCC), recipient of the 2007 Nobel Peace Prize, gives us one of the clearest pictures of what the future may look like. Their Fourth Assessment Report, which is available both in its entirety and in summary on the group's website (www.ipcc.ch), provides a sobering outlook.[28] Recent years have been among the warmest on record, the sea level is rising, and around the world glaciers are in retreat. Extreme weather will become more common.

Precipitation patterns are changing, with more droughts and more flooding. According to the IPCC, it's more than 90 percent likely that these changes are the result of human activity. The process has already been set in motion and is not something that can be quickly halted. Even if greenhouse gases were stabilized today, warming and sea level rise would continue for centuries. However the choices we make today will determine how extreme the problem becomes.

Regardless of our ability to offset or reduce greenhouse-gas emissions, we must prepare for a different future. The poor are in the most vulnerable position because ability to adapt is directly related to social and economic development. With our divine charge to care for the poor, Christians should be particularly concerned about climate change.

The report of Working Group II of the IPCC goes into detail on the specific impacts of warming, showing that the poor will bear the brunt of the negative effects, despite the fact that they have had the least to do with creating the situation. Water availability is expected to increase in high latitudes, but to decrease by 10 to 30 percent in the dry tropics and dry mid-latitudes. In Africa, where access to water is already a critical issue, between 75 and 250 million people are projected to face increased water stress by the year 2020, barely ten years from now.

In some countries, yields from rain-fed agriculture could be reduced by up to 50 percent. Those too poor to irrigate their land will face the worst suffering—essentially a death sentence for a huge number of people who rely on the predictability of rainfall for their livelihoods.

As growing seasons shorten, crop production will fall in Africa, Latin America, and Central and South Asia. Millions will face severe flooding, especially in the poor and heavily populated mega-deltas of Asia and Africa. Disease and malnutrition will increase, while significant percentages of plant and animal species will face extinction. Those of us involved in humanitarian relief and development will have more work, but fewer remedies.

Some of the early impacts are already being felt. Stan Doerr, executive director of ECHO, which works with poor farmers around the world, recently told me, "It is clear to anyone working in small-scale agriculture that the rules have all changed."

Indigenous knowledge that has been built up and treasured since time immemorial is suddenly worthless. One of the most poignant stories of this cultural disaster is included in the sidebar by Dr. Paul Robinson of Wheaton College.

But Dr. Robinson's is not an isolated story. One farmer in Oaxaca explained how he first noticed that droughts were becoming more frequent. He watched a nearby lake slowly dry up over the course of about ten years. Then bark beetles killed the trees, and forest fires became a constant threat. In isolation, none of these events would be clear evidence of a changing climate. But there is an eerie consistency to the accounts from around the world.

A moral response involves both adaptation and mitigation. Global warming is inevitable; climate change cannot be stopped. We must prepare for it and help the poor and vulnerable prepare with more resilient crops, better water storage, and stronger social services, such as access to microcredit and healthcare.

At the same time, our lifestyle choices have significant impact on the magnitude and rate of climate change and, in turn, on the lives of millions of those whom Jesus calls us to protect.

Our Response

Creation is groaning—whether in birth pangs, as Paul describes in Romans 8, or in death throes, I am not sure, but we live on a deeply troubled planet. And yet this crisis seems to have little effect on our daily lives. We still seem to believe we can buy our way out of these problems. Drought, for example, which would be responsible for thousands of deaths in other parts of the world, barely registers in our minds. We may pay a bit more on our water bill but then most of us forget about it.

When we do realize the seriousness of our situation, there are two tempting and equally wrong responses.

One approach tends toward despair. The full weight of what is going on in the world is frightening on a scale that is difficult to comprehend.

The other tendency is to put our heads in the sand and hope the problem will go away. That is the approach the media tends to support—not because it doesn't report on environmental issues, but because their reporting tends to be sporadic and without context, making it difficult for most people to form a coherent picture.

Only Christ can offer the third approach, and that is one of informed hope. Without Christ, our situation is hopeless. With him we can look at what is taking place, assess it realistically, and move forward to respond.

Jesus has given us something to offer the rest of the world, which is trapped in denial or despair. Through him, we can meet one of the environmental movement's greatest needs: hope.

CHAPTER 8

In Our Own Backyards

Almost twenty years ago I took a hot-air balloon ride, sipping champagne as I floated over million-dollar homes, watching the sun set over the Pacific Ocean on a glorious San Diego evening. Six of us had taken off from a spot just south of Rancho Santa Fe, one of the wealthiest neighborhoods in the United States, and drifted slowly south and east, enjoying the best of the Southern California summer. I was about as content as one could be.

At dusk we landed in a field in the hills east of town. As we walked to meet the chase vehicles in the gathering dark, we found ourselves in a small village. Wooden shanties without electricity stood among the oak trees and sagebrush. Women called their children to dinner in Spanish, while young men regarded us silently as we trod the path that served as their main street.

I didn't realize it at the time, but I was seeing the impact of southern Mexico's environmental issues in my own backyard. Deforestation and soil erosion in their homeland had contributed to a lack of opportunity for these people, who now lived in illegal shantytowns in the shadow of some of the richest neighborhoods on this earth.

People frequently ask me how we can choose between caring for the poor and caring for creation, as if they are mutually exclusive. The question surprises me, because my own concern for the earth grew directly out of a concern for the poor. It is true that our immediate convenience often comes into conflict with the long-term needs of creation. Occasionally, legitimate human needs conflict with what is best for another species or an ecosystem. But more often than not, care of the environment lines up with the long-term needs of people.

The environmental movement has something of an image problem, having been often identified with white, upper-middle-class concerns, frequently to the neglect of working people and minorities. As someone told me recently, creation care seems like a cause for bored Americans who want to raise chickens their backyard. It's true that the poor don't have the luxury of worrying about saving polar bears or even their own environment. But somehow we've come to believe that environmental issues are primarily aesthetic, having little to do with food, water, or health. Nothing could be further from the truth.

Poor people are constantly exposed to the effects of environmental degradation, whether through drought induced by climate change, chronic diarrhea due to contaminated water, malaria epidemics exacerbated by deforestation, or myriad other examples. Any response to the needs of poor people that hopes to be sustainable must consider the environment. Conversely, any sustainable conservation effort must consider the needs of the poor. People and creation are part of the same system and are intimately connected. If you hurt one, you hurt the other.

Affluent Americans have been shielded from the consequences of our environmental decisions. If water is scarce or contaminated, we can pay to pipe it across the country and purify it. If soil is degraded, we can pay for fertilizers and amendments. We can afford to move our garbage and waste out of our sight. The cost of seafood may go up, but we can still find our favorite delicacies—or they'll be replaced by substitutes from another part of the world, and before long we'll have forgotten the difference. Because many of us are buffered from direct feedback, we tend to forget that the environment is our life-support system.

Environmental Justice

Even in the United States, the poor, the marginalized, and people of color are far more likely to be exposed to environmental degradation and its consequences. We saw this demonstrated graphically during Hurricane Katrina. However, there are many other ways that the poor disproportionately feel the impacts of our environmental sins.

Leroy Barber, leader of Mission Year, recently gave a presentation in which he contrasted the "Not in My Backyard" attitude of many wealthy communities with his own reality in Atlanta: "It's All in My Backyard." He took his listeners on a virtual tour of his neighborhood, pointing out the junkyards, dumps, hazardous chemicals, and a prison, all within a two-block radius of his home.[1] Far from the exception, this is the rule for many poor neighborhoods.

To a startling degree, exposure to environmental hazards falls along racial lines. In the 1980s interest in the connections between poverty, race, and environmental issues grew in the United States, and with that interest came a host of studies that confirmed a direct link. There is a dramatic statistical correlation between race and proximity to facilities where hazardous waste is treated, stored, and disposed of.

As someone who would like to believe our society has made great strides in putting racism behind us, this reality was difficult for me to acknowledge. Terms like *environmental racism* do not come easily to me. But the data is convincing. In 1990 more than 43 percent of the people living within one mile of these facilities were persons of color, although people of color made up just 24 percent of the general populace.[2] Race has been shown to be a more important predictor of the location of toxic waste facilities than poverty or land value.[3]

Air quality in the inner cities is likely to be as much as five times worse than in suburban neighborhoods. As a result, African American and Puerto Rican children are six times more likely to die of asthma than white children.[4]

A Broken Promise

Two decades ago, I took care of a young girl in the emergency room. It was a hot summer day, and Etta was having a severe asthma attack. I promised her I would not let her die.

Etta was not my first asthma patient, nor would she be my last. In the past twenty years, asthma rates among children under age four have more than doubled. Ask school kids today if either they or their classmates have asthma, and the answer will be yes. Poor kids are hardest hit: a recent study indicates that one quarter of the children in Harlem have asthma, which is more than three times the national average.

One reason for this increase in childhood asthma is air pollution, especially in inner cities. Numerous studies have demonstrated that asthma admissions to hospitals increase as ground-level ozone and particulate matter rises. That's why we have "ozone alerts" that warn susceptible inner-city children and the elderly to stay inside on hot, muggy days.

What would happen if ground-level ozone levels were reduced? Would acute asthma events also decrease? The 1996 Olympic Games in Atlanta provided a unique opportunity to study this question.

To reduce traffic congestion during the games, the city of Atlanta closed the downtown area to car traffic, increased access to public transportation through additional buses and trains, and promoted flexible work schedules, carpooling, and telecommuting for Atlanta workers. The result: for seventeen days, peak daily ozone concentrations decreased 28 percent. Concurrently, acute asthma events dropped as much as 44 percent. Atlanta's inner-city children on Medicaid seemed to benefit the most, showing a more than 40 percent decrease in asthma-related emergency-room visits. After the Olympics, when Atlanta traffic patterns returned to normal, so did asthma visits and admissions.

On that hot summer day in an inner-city emergency room, I was unable to keep my promise to Etta. She was killed by an asthma attack exacerbated by air pollution. But I am trying to keep my promise to God. He wants everyone to have access to clean air. Riding a bike, taking the subway, and carpooling are ways we can all demonstrate our love for the Creator, his creation, and all our global neighbors.

Matthew Sleeth, MD, is author of *Serve God, Save the Planet* (Zondervan 2007) and executive director of Blessed Earth (www.blessed-earth.org).

Risk of cancer is shown to be much higher as well. A recent EPA study showed the risk of contracting cancer as a result of air pollution to be thirty-five times higher in Los Angeles than the national average.[5]

Although great strides have been made in lowering the incidence of lead poisoning—one of the most significant environmental health threats for children—success is not equally distributed. African American children are twice as likely to suffer from lead poisoning as white children.[6]

But environmental injustice in the United States isn't confined to the inner cities. Mountaintop-removal coal mining is another example of how the needs of the poor, the marginalized, and creation are overlooked or ignored to satisfy our convenience and the greed of the few. This relatively new type of mining uses explosives to flatten whole mountains to get at the coal seams within. It is cheaper than traditional coal mining—but devastating for both communities and the environment. After trees are cleared, the top eight hundred feet of a mountain is removed by blasting, then pushed into the neighboring canyons and streams. It is estimated that more than a thousand miles of Appalachian streams were buried between 1985 and 2001. By 2010, a projected 1.4 million acres of a forest that has stood for millennia will be forever destroyed.[7]

Not only does this type of mining devastate the integrity and legacy of the mountain ecosystems, it affects property values, heritage, and the health of those downstream. This method is designed to save labor, therefore it provides few jobs and little economic benefit to those it hurts most. The areas where it is practiced are among the poorest in the United States. They also contain some of the most biodiverse temperate forests in the world.

Fortunately, this is one problem where the church has been a leader. Among the most important opponents of this practice have been Christian voices, including an organization called Christians for the Mountains led by Allen Johnson.[8]

When we learn of what is being done in the hills of West Virginia, Kentucky, and Tennessee, it's easy to become righteously indignant. Yet our quest for cheap energy and our resistance to change is subsidizing it. At the website www.Ilovemountains.org, which partners with Christians for the Mountains, I entered my own zip code and was able to see current satellite photos of the mountains that were decapitated in order to keep my lights on and my computer charged.

Immigration

The ravaged mountain in Kentucky is not the only environmental justice issue with a direct link to my neighborhood. Half a mile from my house in San Diego, several hundred migrant workers line up every morning, hoping to find work. A few miles farther south, the city of Tijuana is booming, expanding ever eastward as more and more people arrive at the border. Some of them are on their way into the United States; many others never make it any farther than Tijuana.

Why are these workers leaving their loved ones behind and risking death, arrest, and deportation to look for work elsewhere? Why have they come to our backyards, figuratively and literally? Because people will do almost anything to feed their families and provide for their children. Because desperate people do desperate things. Unlike the negative stereotypes they are often given, these are for the most part entrepreneurial, capable people, enduring incredible hardship for the sake of their families back home.

Reactions to the problem are varied. Local churches regularly send teams of youth and families to Tijuana to build homes for migrants. North of the border, many Christians see only that these immigrants have violated the law by crossing the border. There's even a segment of the environmental community that has taken a xenophobic stance, directly blaming immigrants for environmental degradation and other problems, reinforcing environmentalism's elitist stereotype. Some have gone so far as to say that the increased standard of living these workers would experience in the United States will increase their environmental footprint—and is, therefore, sufficient reason to keep them out.[9] The argument is, in effect, that the world can't afford more Americans. But very few are practicing upstream thinking, asking why these people have come here in the first place.

Looking for a way to increase the local impact of our work, Plant With Purpose researched the root causes of emigration from Mexico. Most immigrants came from small mountain villages where firewood and charcoal were among the principle economic products—places like the town of La Muralla, which we encountered in chapter 2. Deforestation and land degradation is so bad in this region that one United Nations report called the state of Oaxaca the most eroded spot on earth.[10]

Most of these people would prefer to stay at home, to keep their families intact, and to live within their own culture. But environmental issues such as deforestation and soil erosion force them to seek opportunities elsewhere. In the book *Endangered Mexico,* author Joel Simon talks to Oaxacan farmers about why they emigrate: "Time after time," Simon writes, "I heard the same refrain, '*Porque la tierra ya no da,*' because the earth no longer gives."[11]

What happens on the hillsides of Mexico—or in Somalia or China for that matter—has a direct impact on our own communities and churches. *Porque la tierra ya no da,* people are lining up to look for work in many neighborhoods and forming impromptu villages in the hills behind our cities. And what we observe is just the tip of the iceberg.

Environmental migration is drawing the attention of scholars and national security analysts. The term *environmental refugee,*

We Shall Overcome

Most mornings I get the opportunity to walk to my office. As I walk, I often feel like I am surveying the damage from a storm the night before—only this is a storm of habits, vices, and poverty. I see condoms left on the ground, and cans and bottles of malt liquor that have been thrown from cars. Coming out of my house two weeks ago, I found my car window busted. On my walk last week, a neighbor called out to me that her window had been broken as well. Over the last month there have been two cars stolen and numerous break-ins.

It seems that the evil that won't show itself during the day gets free reign at night while we sleep, and in the morning we're left to survey the damage. We come out to find cars missing or evidence of a woman having given herself to some guy for ten bucks in the backseat of a car next to our house.

On my walks to work in the mornings, I've begun to pray that somehow the light of day will break through the storms of evil that rule during the night. I pray that lost hope would be restored. I do this to fight the voice inside that keeps gently pushing me to leave this place or to give up hope. "Why are you doing this?" it whispers. "Why are you living here? Why are you even walking? It's not like you're going to save the environment."

Environmentalists, people who were once a joke to me, are now some of my favorite people. They have taught me that a clean environment is vital to the health of a neighborhood like mine. Similar to the litter I see on the ground as I walk, the air I breathe is also polluted—I just can't see it. Vehicle emissions and the harmful chemicals put out by local factories fill the air, and smog levels are disproportionately higher in neighborhoods like mine.

Each morning I feel that battle within me, but as I pray I am encouraged to continue. I think about our Mission Year team members who live in neighborhoods like mine around the country, and I pray for their work to bring light. Hope ultimately wins out, although some mornings just barely, and I choose to hope one more day.

The world around me gives me every excuse to stop hoping and to live for myself. The tension within that says, "It's not worth it," is matched by the pull of individualism that tells me to take care of myself and get my family out. But the Scriptures give me every reason to stay, fight, and insist that hope will not disappoint.

Wherever we are, we can offer alternatives to suffering alone in this hurting world. Will you join us on this journey? Will you pray each evening that light will overcome the evils of the darkness? Will you drive less, walk more, and remember the neighborhoods filled with people who are suffering?

With your help we will not be not overcome by evil, but we will overcome evil with good.

Leroy Barber is president of Mission Year.

originally coined by Lester Brown, is gaining currency. According to Norman Myers, as many as twenty-five million environmental refugees existed in 1995, and by 1999 there were more environmental refugees than traditional refugees fleeing oppression or persecution.[12]

In a similar way, linkages between environmental degradation and human trafficking are gaining attention. Modern-day slavery is rampant, affecting an estimated twenty-seven million people today—more than at the height of the trans-Atlantic slave trade.[13] Christians are becoming passionate about this issue, and several organizations are helping to expose the horrors of slavery, enforce the laws, and free the victims. But upstream, the root problem is desperation, frequently with roots in environmental degradation. People who cannot make a living on degraded land are forced to do desperate things, such as giving or selling their children into slavery. In Thailand, rural girls from marginalized hill tribes frequently end up in the brothels of Bangkok and Phuket.

Unless we practice upstream thinking—looking at root causes rather than merely symptoms—it can be easy to miss the connections between tropical deforestation and migration, illegal immigration, and human slavery. We have to work through several steps to see how one seemingly minor problem—deforestation—can contribute to an injustice as ugly as sex trafficking. Yet we must.

We must make the connection between creation care and justice if we want to have an impact on the problems of the poor and oppressed in our own country and around the world. Environmental problems and their solutions transcend race, border, and economic class, and yet we must not ignore the disproportionate impact these problems have on economically disadvantaged and marginalized communities. Any comprehensive creation-care program must respond to the needs of the poor and the marginalized—working alongside them to clean up their neighborhoods, fight their oppressors, protect their reefs, preserve their rivers, and replant their forests.

Taking care of creation isn't just about saving the whales or the spotted owl (although these concerns are far more important than the skeptics would have us believe). Creation care isn't just about *reduce, reuse, recycle*. And it certainly isn't about keeping others out or exporting our own environmental problems to other countries so America can remain pristine. It is about preserving creatures and conserving wilderness, but it is also about saving neighborhoods from our waste, and improving the health and safety of children who live there. It is about working for justice for poor families in Appalachia and collaborating with poor farmers around the world who are struggling to produce food under increasingly difficult circumstances. Justice for the poor and oppressed should be a seamless part of creation care, just as creation care is fundamental to proclaiming and demonstrating God's kingdom to all of creation.

CHAPTER 9

Creation Care: The Time Has Come

One blustery Sunday morning I walked down the beach near my home in San Diego. The salt air and crashing surf called me to play, but I had a task. Carrying a big garbage bag, I stopped every few feet to pick up a bit of trash and put it in my sack. I found a lot of plastic along the tide line, where the sea had washed it in along with bits of kelp and sea grass. Cigarette butts and fast-food packaging littered the sea wall.

A few paces ahead, my children—Danny, age five, and Amanda, eight—collected most of the big pieces. Danny proudly showed me the broken flip-flop he recovered.

A little farther down the beach, other families from our church were doing the same thing. It was an extension of our worship service where, as our pastor said, we gathered to praise God before scattering to serve our community and God's creation.

Despite the fact that the beach looked clean when we arrived, we collected a substantial amount of plastic, Styrofoam, paper, and metal. Along the way we enjoyed some wonderful conversations with people we met on the beach and had a chance to share with our community our concern for God's creation.

Our small Presbyterian congregation is hardly on the cutting edge. Yet we went to the beach that Sunday morning to extend our worship into action. Baby steps.

Biblical Basis

Creation care isn't a new idea. The story of our relationship with God's creation runs throughout the Bible. I came to this field as a bit of a skeptic, and the first few times I saw lists of Scripture verses related to creation care or environmental stewardship, they seemed contrived. Today, the emphasis seems obvious. Others have done more thorough exegesis of the Scripture behind creation care than I have space to do here, but it is worthwhile to look at some of the highlights.

The biblical account is not just the story of God's love for his people and the redemption of humankind through Christ. It is that, but is also the story of God's love for everything he has made. We humans are an important part of it, but *all* of creation is involved.

Like many young evangelicals, I was taught to substitute my own name into John 3:16: "For God so loved *Scott* that he gave his only begotten Son . . ." While this tells an important truth about God's love, it is less than the whole truth. I was substituting my name for the word *kosmos*. *Kosmos* means all that God created; the universe.[1] "For God so loved *all that he made* . . ."

The substitution of one's own name in this verse results in a self-centered gospel, focused on personal salvation above all else. But God's love extends to the entire creation.

When God created the first humans and placed them in the garden, it was to serve *(abad)* and protect *(shamar)* the garden (Genesis 2:15).[2] (These words have also been translated as "to work" and "to keep.") The first job humans were given was to be the stewards of all that God created. Later, humans were told to be fruitful and multiply, but that same directive was given to all living creatures. Part of our stewardship should be to make it possible for them to fulfill God's desires.

God places extraordinary importance on land throughout the Old Testament. In Leviticus there are explicit instructions on how to take care of the land, including giving it a Sabbath rest every seven years. If the Sabbath is not observed, the Bible says the land will take its own rest (Leviticus 26:34-35).

In Job 38 through 41, when Job calls God to account for what has happened to him, God responds by speaking about creation. God tells Job that there are many things Job doesn't understand and that aren't for Job to understand. But in God's response, we get a glimpse of God's relationship with creation. We see God's interaction with natural forces as well as with creatures great and small—creatures that have nothing to do with people and their needs.

The story is not always about us. God's words in Job 38:4-7 make that quite plain:

> Where were you when I laid the earth's foundation?
> Tell me, if you understand. . . .
> On what were its footings set,
> or who laid its cornerstone—
> while the morning stars sang together
> and all the angels shouted for joy?

It is clear in this passage that God takes delight in these things, that they are a source of joy. He talks about the mountain goats, the lion, the wild donkey, the raven, the hawk, and the eagle. "Tell me if you understand," he says to Job.

This passage also demonstrates the glory of God. As majestic and wondrous as these things are, they are nothing compared to the One who created them and understands their inner workings.

When Job and his friends presumed to speak for God, as we still do all too often, God answered by pointing to creation. I can imagine a similar scene taking place today, with us shamefacedly having to answer, "No, we don't know where the wild goat gives birth. We killed them all before we found out."

The Psalms are full of references to creation. Psalm 24 reminds us that it belongs to God and glorifies him. The earth is the Lord's. Nowhere is it given to humans. Psalm 104 talks about how God lovingly provides for his creatures, whereas Psalm 148 commands them to give him praise.

The Creation Care Adventure

It all started with a voice crying in the wilderness. His message was not too different from the words of the misfit prophet who cleared the way for Jesus: "We've got to change our ways or there's destruction coming."

This retired environmental scientist made many friends as he enthusiastically and persistently presented his case for creation care. Slowly I came to realize that God is not only keen to save souls; he is also committed to save the planet on which those souls live.

He pointed out that all our earnest efforts to bring new life to an impoverished tribe in the desert of Ethiopia, for instance, would come to naught if a warming earth causes the sea level to rise and inundate the desert, wiping out all our community development projects. Hmmm. Maybe there is a direct connection between these two interests of our life-saving God!

Gathering other converts to the cause, we formed a team that explained the creation-care imperative to our church. One Sunday,

---

Isaiah and the other prophets link restoration of the land with God's favor and the coming of God's kingdom, the same kingdom we have been called to proclaim and to foreshadow in our relationships. In Isaiah 41, God draws the connection between poverty and deforestation and resolves both of them together.

The theme of creation care is not abandoned in the New Testament. Caring for the earth is covered in Jesus' reminder to love our neighbors. Knowing that our neighbor's well-being is dependent on creation, this simple call offers sufficient justification for creation care. If I love God, I will treat his gifts and the work of his hands with respect. And if I love my neighbor, I will ensure that I live in a way that doesn't limit my neighbor's access to the basic resources that he or she needs to survive: water, air, and land.

the local power company gave away energy-saving CFL light bulbs and signed people up for home energy audits. Another Sunday the folks in our church who owned hybrid cars parked them on the patio and touted their benefits. (I'm driving one today because of their testimonies!) We mounted a campaign to replace plastic bottles and bags, had sturdy cloth bags and stainless steel bottles imprinted with our CC logo, and sold 1,200 bags after worship.

Because our community is environmentally concerned, we have reached out to our city council, providing money and volunteers for renovation projects of local lagoons. We even received a commendation from the mayor at a city council meeting.

We see the creation-care initiative as part of our evangelistic strategy as we demonstrate the relevance the gospel, in word and deed, to the concerns of our neighbors. We have a ball with our electronic waste days, preservation of species petitions, lagoon clean-up projects, and more. Most importantly, I think our Creator-Savior is pleased.

Tom Theriault is outreach pastor at Solana Beach Presbyterian Church in California.

There are also specific reminders of creation in the New Testament. For example, in Luke 12:6-7, while teaching the disciples of their value, Jesus tells us God remembers every sparrow. Although humans are more valuable, the God of the universe considers sparrows to be important too.

The apostle Paul says creation is groaning, waiting for the children of God to be revealed (Romans 8:22). All creation eagerly anticipates the good news we carry. How do we live out the gospel so that it is in fact good news for creation?

Colossians 1:16 reminds us that "all things were created by him [Jesus] and for him." This flies in the face of our self-centered pop theology that tells us all things were created for our enjoyment—and that we'd better use them up before they burn.

Revelation contains an often overlooked verse in which God proclaims that the time has come for destroying those who destroy the earth (11:18). Thankfully that is not the end of the story, for Revelation ends by revisiting the garden. Once again the Tree of Life is seen, framing the entire biblical narrative, and "the leaves of the tree are for the healing of the nations" (22:2).

In popular eschatology the earth is burned up. Yet as Steven Bouma-Prediger has pointed out, the verse from which that doctrine is derived, 2 Peter 3:10, is often mistranslated. Properly translated, that passage states that the earth will be found or judged, and it gives the image of a new heaven and a new earth. This speaks of the redemption and purification of heaven and earth, not starting over.[3] Earth will be renewed and restored, not burned up and thrown away.

Regardless of how the end times ultimately transpire, we would do well to honor God's commands and faithfully steward that which God created and loves.

History

Throughout history, there is a remarkable legacy of Christians who have taken God's call to stewardship seriously, working and keeping the garden. Perhaps the best known is St. Francis, who considered all of creation his family. Even sun and moon were brother and sister, with the same heavenly Father. All are given the sacred task of praising the Creator. In the Great Commission call to "Go into all the world and preach the good news to all creation" (Mark 16:15), St. Francis heard good news not just for humanity, but for every part of creation.

He is by no means alone. If we look a little deeper, we find many people in historical Christianity whose voices remind us of the importance of creation as God's general revelation. St. Augustine said, "Some people, in order to discover God, read books. But there is a great book; the very appearance of created things. Look about you! Look below you! Note it. Read it. God, whom you want to discover, never wrote that book with ink. Instead He set before your eyes the things He had made. Can you ask for a louder voice than that?"[4]

St. Thomas Aquinas warned that "any error about creation also leads to an error about God."[5]

John Wesley admonished his listeners on the importance of our stewardship role, saying, "By acquainting ourselves with subjects in natural philosophy, we enter into a kind of association with nature's words, and unite in the general concert of her extensive choir. By thus acquainting and familiarizing ourselves with the words of nature, we become as it were a member of her family, a participant in her felicities; but while we remain ignorant, we are like strangers and sojourners in a foreign land, unknowing and unknown."[6]

William Wilberforce has gained renewed recognition for his role in the abolition of the slave trade because of the movie *Amazing Grace*. But he was also instrumental in founding the Royal Society for the Prevention of Cruelty to Animals, the first animal-welfare organization in the world, proving that one need not choose between seeking justice for people or for animals.[7]

William Carey, the great missionary to India, is known as the father of modern missions.[8] He may also be the father of environmental missions. He worked to improve India's soils and wrote on forestry, advocating for forest conservation and reforestation in India.[9] An avid botanist, he recognized the bounty God had given to India in the form of its plant life, taking an interest in it when few others did. He spent much of his time collecting, cataloging, and growing hundreds of species of plants, in which he took great delight. This led him to found the Agri-Horticultural Society of India, which functioned for many years as the agricultural department of the Indian government and still exists today.[10] Carey was also a tremendous advocate for justice, working to abolish the caste system and end the practice of burning widows alive. None of this got in the way of his work of proclaiming the gospel; instead, these efforts served to complement it and strengthen his legacy and witness for subsequent generations.

George Washington Carver is famous for researching the peanut and sweet potato and championing them to rebuild depleted soils and assist poor farmers in the war-devastated southern United States. Believing that science revealed the truth about God, he encouraged people to study creation in order to learn more about God, seeing this as a form of witness. He said, "To me, Nature . . . is the little windows through which God permits me to commune with Him, and to see much of His glory, by simply lifting the curtain and looking in. I love to think of Nature as wireless telegraph stations through which God speaks to us every day, every hour, and every moment of our lives."[11] In his study of creation Carver noticed the virtuous cycles that God has embedded throughout nature, bringing life from death again and again. He encouraged farmers to mimic those cycles, putting their waste products to productive uses.

These heroes of the faith provide inspiration to us today at Plant With Purpose. We could do few things that would be better than continuing their legacy as bearers of the good news.

Creation Care Today

In more recent times, many of God's people have lost sight of their stewardship role. When I first became involved in the Christian environmental movement in the mid-1990s, voices were few and the audience skeptical. However, I felt that if other American Christians could see what I had seen, their attitudes would be different. I noticed a deeper understanding of the importance of creation care on the mission field and among Christians in the developing world who were not burdened with American political prejudices.

One of the pioneers of the Christian and particularly evangelical environmental awakening was Dr. Calvin DeWitt, of the University of Wisconsin, founder of the Au Sable Institute of Environmental Studies, who combines understanding of ecology with deep faith and an infectious sense of wonder. In the early 1990s, he and some others, including the Evangelical Environmental Network (EEN), brought together a group of Christian leaders with an interest in creation. Plant With Purpose's mission drew enough notice that I was invited, despite my lack of credentials.

At those first meetings biology professors from Christian colleges tended to be overrepresented, and there were very few pastors. But in the years since, courageous individuals like Peter Illyn at Restoring Eden and Jim Ball at EEN have been tireless in their efforts to rouse the church. In the last couple of years, a broader group of people has at last awakened to the call to stewardship.

Today, there is a groundswell of people within the church who see creation care as a vital part of their walk with Christ. Matthew Sleeth, for example, uses his experience as an emergency-room physician to share with others the connection between health and the environment. He, his wife, Nancy, and their family have become role models of sustainable living. They demonstrate the type of stewardship that can truly change the world. Other organizations such as A Rocha, Care of Creation, and Flourish have found an audience.

Some pastors have finally begun to make creation care a priority, including Tri Robinson at Vineyard Boise in Idaho and Joel Hunter at Northland, A Church Distributed near Orlando. Both have been outspoken on the topic and have active creation-care ministries in their congregations.

Vineyard Boise, for example, cultivates a large organic garden on its church property, maintained by more than a hundred volunteers. Produce is used to feed the needy and homeless. Last year they provided over 20,000 pounds of fresh vegetables to more than 1,300 families.[12] This church's work serves as inspiration for dozens of other churches that are taking remarkable and creative steps toward creation care and stewardship of the earth. My own congregation near San Diego is hoping to follow Vineyard Boise's example as we collaborate with the church across the street on a community garden, where organic produce will feed the poor.

Interest in creation care has seen tremendous growth among youth and younger Christians. Several years ago, as I was speaking to different groups, I noticed that audiences in their twenties were quite receptive and even welcomed the idea of "planting trees

Becoming a Creation Care Congregation

When we embarked on our journey as a church to embrace creation care as part of our regular ministry, we had no idea the impact it would have on our church as a whole. We began taking a more active role in caring for the environment simply because we recognized it as something God says to do in his Word. But the impact has been far reaching:

From Bystanders to Involved People

Many in our church were already working in environmental-type businesses. From the fields of conservation to biology, people were excited about the opportunity to meld their expertise with the value of caring for creation. These people were simply waiting for the church to tell them it was okay.

Increasing Social Consciousness

Our creation-care ministry enabled us to help bring awareness to areas of need—and helped us discover connections between environmental issues and other human concerns.

For example, when Hurricane Katrina hit the Gulf Coast, our ministry funded outreach teams to New Orleans through funds

for Jesus." But the feedback I received from older audiences could be summarized as "We love the economic development work you are doing, but we don't get the trees."

When I met with Christian foundations, I often felt I was dragging an environmental liability behind me. The director of one foundation began the conversation by saying, "I hope you're not one of those guys who's going to try to convince me trees are as important to God as people."

"No," I said. "But I will tell you that people need trees." He began to listen.

raised from recycled cell phones. The crisis of human trafficking became another focus for our church, particularly as we discovered how closely this crisis was connected to the environment. We learned that some of the African children forced into sex slavery were being captured as they made the daily two-mile walk to the nearest fresh water source. Dire circumstances of poverty due to drought or famine created other situations where traffickers could prey on desperately poor parents, who were willing to sell one child to traffickers just to get money to feed their other children—never realizing they would never hear from that child again.

Connecting with Curious Seekers

One of the most surprising impacts of this ministry has been the opportunities it has presented to build bridges into the world and share the gospel. Whether it's through our people serving in local environmental projects or speaking about biblical solutions for a world in crisis on secular college campuses, God has given us many opportunities to take his message of redemption, love, and grace to a world in desperate need of it.

Tri Robinson is the author of *Saving God's Green Earth* (Ampelon, 2006) and senior pastor of the Boise Vineyard Church, a fellowship of two thousand people in Boise, Idaho.

With younger people, I rarely have to explain the environmental aspects. They get it—and embrace it. Today there is a growing movement on college campuses, and people like Ben Lowe and Anna Jane Joyner with Renewal are mobilizing Christian college campuses around the country.

However, much work remains to be done. Environmental ministries are not mainstream in most churches or in the minds of most Christians. Recently I addressed a half-empty workshop at a large, well-attended conference. If the truth were known, I believe that room would have been overflowing; packed with

Christians eager to learn what could be done to restore creation. They would be competing for space with environmentalists coming to learn about the hope we have in Christ.

There are a number of reasons creation care is not central. For one thing, it requires an upstream mind-set. We usually focus on quick fixes and Band-Aids rather than root causes.

Humans tend to be reactive rather than proactive. This is why most of our healthcare spending is on treatment rather than prevention. When we address issues of water, we drill wells, which is good—but that solution will not last unless we take into account the health of the watershed.

According to a recent *Foreign Affairs* article, the United States has spent twenty times more money on food aid in Africa than on agricultural development.[13] A similar mindset explains why Haitian farmers cut down trees for immediate survival even when they know the long-term health of the land requires forests. Part of human nature is that we tend to be short-sighted and driven by the need for quick results.

There is also the denial-or-despair response. These are big problems, and we wonder what can one person do about them. So we do nothing.

Finally, there are a couple of myths that are widely believed within the church. The first myth is that environmental awareness will cause people to worship the creation instead of the Creator. I find this puzzling, because wilderness and nature have the opposite effect on me. My involvement in environmental issues has taught me about the incredible intricacy and complexity of God's creation, reminding me of God's attributes and my own humble place in the world. "What is man that you are mindful of him?" (Psalm 8:4).

It's no surprise that many people become Christians at camp, where they learn of God's love for them and can look up and see that "the heavens declare the glory of God" (Psalm 19:1). Paul tells us that creation provides enough evidence of God to leave us without excuse (Romans 1:20). I have never met a Christian who felt the slightest temptation to worship creation. It certainly didn't seem to be a fear George Washington Carver grappled with as he encouraged people to learn about God through nature.

On the contrary, I have met many Christian biologists and ecologists who have helped me to rediscover awe and wonder in creation and to see the signature of the Creator in unexpected places. I was surprised to discover how consistently they employed Scripture in seeking to understand our role in taking care of the earth.

I suspect that the fear may be less that we will begin to worship creation and more that we may forsake the idols of our society which have often co-opted the church. One of the greatest temptations we face in our culture is to worship our own technological, architectural, and economic achievements. As a society we believe we can improve on creation—that we are, in effect, better than God. Just as in the days of Babel, we've set up our own achievements as something to replace God's achievements. Virtual reality replaces God's reality. Human-engineered beauty replaces the beauty God created. Unfettered growth replaces justice.

Insofar as the church has been seduced by the prevailing culture, we have bought into the same worldview. As Christians begin to value and take care of creation, we break from the orthodoxy of our culture and its idols of technology, consumption, and unrestrained growth.

Another myth is that deep down, at the root of all this talk about caring for the creation, there is some political agenda. It's true that there are policy issues with immense bearing on the health of creation, which should be taken seriously. However, much of what is going on around the globe transcends politics or defies easy political classification.

For example, environmentalism is often depicted as being against private property. Yet at Plant With Purpose we advocate for property rights. Giving people ownership and a stake in their communities is critical. Poor farmers who have the right to use wood and products from trees they plant will be much more likely to care for them. Similarly, farmers are more effective stewards of land they are assured of being able to use in the future. A renter has very little stake in his or her property. Thus, one of the most effective uses of loans in Haiti has been the purchase of land. Successful conservation or environmental restoration projects always have a strong degree of local ownership and community participation. On the other hand, within the very communal Mixteco culture of Oaxaca, Mexico, it makes more sense to emphasize collective responses and community action.

There is a role for government too. Where local rights are threatened, government protection is essential. Government can either create or reduce subsidies, changing economic incentives to create a more sustainable economy. The Dominican subsidy on propane for home cooking, for example, has had much to do with the reduction of the use of firewood and has been credited for the comparatively better health of the Dominican forest.[14]

When issues transcend national boundaries, international treaties and laws make sense. Examples include climate change, fisheries management, and trade in endangered species. Internationally we must work to avoid exporting our pollution problems and environmental issues to other countries due to uneven laws and enforcement.

No one political party has a monopoly on environmental responsibility. Americans do not have to change party affiliations to be good stewards and creation-care advocates. Environmental stewardship requires flexible and practical legislation together with a great deal of individual initiative, responsibility, and leadership. If these are not joined together, even the best legislation will not solve our environmental crisis.

There are dozens of lifestyle choices we can make that have nothing to do with politics. All of us can live more simply, drive less, use less water and electricity, recycle, and buy locally grown food. In our churches we can bring attention to the scriptural basis for stewardship. We can encourage our workplaces to reduce consumption and waste. And organizations such as Plant With Purpose can provide opportunities for people of all political persuasions to make a difference.

The idea that stewardship and conservation are part of a liberal agenda seems ludicrous in much of the developing world. I remember the shock on the face of our Dominican director when

I tried to explain the suspicion with which many U.S. churches regarded the environmental aspects of our work. It was a horrifying thought to him that American Christians would be less than enthusiastic about caring for the earth. Many of our brothers and sisters in the developing world are way ahead of us in their understanding of stewardship, and there is much that we can learn from them.

Free of the myths, and filled with the hope Jesus gives us, opportunities for creation care are manifold. Some incredibly creative things are already being done. Many churches now have creation-care committees (or green teams) that are finding ways to get engaged in their communities, to demonstrate their love for their neighbors and God's creation. By showing up in some unexpected places, humble and ready to serve, churches are building bridges to people they would never reach otherwise. By mixing with and working alongside other volunteers to rebuild trails, plant native species in parks, and clean up neighborhoods, Christians are able to share the gospel and make their churches an inviting place to thousands who might never have considered darkening a church's door. The pastors and team members I have talked to indicate that, far from diminishing their witness, environmental stewardship has opened doors to their communities and their neighbors that they had never imagined.

People with a deep hunger for God, who have known him only partially and seen him only through the general revelation of creation, now have the opportunity to be introduced to the God of the Bible. They are delighted to discover that God cares about many of the same things they do, and that the One who created all things offers hope for the redemption and restoration of all.

CHAPTER 10

Getting into the Game

"Daddy, when I grow up, I want to help you save the rainforest." My daughter, Amanda, then five, looked at me with an expression that made me melt. For a fraction of a second I thought we were completely in tune. Then she added, "I could be a butterfly or a fairy and fly around pollinating the trees."

It wasn't quite the kind of help I was looking for, but it does serve to underline an important problem. Once we understand the state of the world and our call to be stewards, what can we do? Where do we start? The problems are vast and often seem so far away.

As each of us considers how to respond to the groaning of creation, there is much that can be learned from Plant With Purpose's story. The entire world faces vicious cycles similar to the one we recognized involving deforestation and poverty. And there are undoubtedly other virtuous cycles that can address two problems with one solution. Each vicious cycle we confront presents an opportunity for a corresponding virtuous cycle.

Two of the biggest problems in the world are environmental degradation and widespread poverty. There are 3.14 billion people living on less than $2.50 a day.[1] If the poor are recognized as a resource rather than an obstacle, can a virtuous cycle be discovered in the midst of this? Is it possible that the poor could become leaders in solving the enormous environmental problems the planet faces?

Van Jones, in his book *The Green Collar Economy: How One Solution Can Fix Our Two Biggest Problems,* makes the case that this is possible in the United States.[2] He advocates putting the unemployed and underemployed to work to create a healthier, more sustainable country. Jobs can be created weatherizing homes, installing solar panels, and improving energy efficiency. As Jones says, we need to do everything we can to aid and encourage business and eco-entrepreneurs to develop market-based solutions to solve environmental problems. This is similar to what Plant With Purpose is doing internationally.

We must also look for opportunities to create smaller virtuous cycles in our environmental and economic solutions. Nature is designed to function as a series of virtuous cycles. But most often, our attempts to address the problems are linear and finite. Recycling is one step toward closing the loop to sustainability—but it is only the beginning.

Solutions must be empowering. Everyone, from the church member in Michigan to the farmer in Haiti, has a role to play. The rural poor must have a role in the stewardship and restoration of the land, and the urban poor must have a role in greening and redeeming their neighborhoods and cities.

Any real solution must take into account both environmental and economic considerations. I once walked miles into a protected national park in Indonesia that was filled with illegal cinnamon plantations and crisscrossed by paths used by illegal loggers to get deeper into the park. The national park was set aside with the best of intentions. But without corresponding changes in the incentives for the people who rely on the land, nothing will change.

The same applies to solutions in the United States. Economic incentives must be aligned with environmental outcomes. At a national level this means changing the way farm subsidies are applied. It means incentives and standards for improved fuel efficiency for cars. It means investment in alternative energies. It also means finding creative ways for local communities to participate in and benefit economically from the health of their surrounding environment.

Finally, any viable solution must have a spiritual dimension, because ultimately the problem is a spiritual one. The church must lead the way, offering the hope we have and setting an example with our own stewardship. We must forsake the wanton consumerism that has overwhelmed our culture and which is ultimately suicidal. And we must offer a healthy alternative based on biblical values of worship, contentment, community, and Sabbath.

Personal Call

How then should we respond as individuals?

First, we as evangelicals need to get over our suspicion of science and learn what we can from it. Unless we understand our environment and how it works, how can we protect it? And we must learn not only from the scientists but also from our brothers and sisters on the front lines: the farmer in Tanzania who can no longer count on the rain, the Gabra elder who can no longer graze his animals, the Haitian family who has seen firsthand the devastation that comes when life-support systems are wiped out.

Second, we in the church should realize how much we have in common with the wider environmental community. They value creation, in part, because they hunger for the Creator. We should engage in dialogue with them, but we must begin with an attitude of humility. We have been absent from the conversation for too long to be brash.

Nonetheless, we have something important to offer: hope in a place where there is a dearth of good news. A former colleague at Plant With Purpose told me he became a Christian partly because of the despair he felt as an environmental-studies major. The problems were too vast. The solutions proposed by science and government were draconian or came up short. As far as he could see, there was no hope for the world, except in Christ. Of course, that is what we believe: that Jesus is the hope for the world.

With all the problems in this world—injustice, poverty, disease, immorality, and more—it can be hard to see hope outside of miraculous intervention from Jesus. However, justice and righteousness will win. In fact we have already won. Like us, creation is dying, but Jesus already gained the victory over death at Calvary.

When I think of how to act on the call to stewardship, I am again reminded of the story of the feeding of the five thousand, this time as related in the book of John. The disciples looked for Jesus to solve the problem, just as we often do. But Jesus' seemingly impossible response was to put the problem back in their hands. Trusting him, they turn to the crowd. A little boy, who perhaps had no hope of making a real difference, came forward with his five loaves and two fish. We can imagine how inadequate, even how foolish, he must have felt. Five loaves and two fish! But in faith he offered what he had. And from these acts of faith, Jesus did something impossible.

But he didn't feed the people without requiring something. First he required the disciples to act on faith, and someone in the crowd offered what he had in obedience. The disciples acted, but they also involved the community in the solution. And both the disciples and the boy had to take action, despite the fact that they could not solve the problem with what they had. I see us in the role of the disciples, and the communities we work with are analogous to the crowd. We must invite them into the process and trust God to multiply what we offer.

What we have to offer may seem so puny in the face of the need that it doesn't seem worth bringing forward. The temptation is to believe we can't make a difference. Yet we must move forward on faith, offering what we have even if it means facing ridicule and looking foolish, because only then will raw material for a miracle be present.

We will be held accountable for what we do with our talents, no matter how inadequate they may seem. With all we have been given in the American church, it is impossible to argue that we are anything other than those who have five talents. We are in the wealthiest nation on earth, with every imaginable opportunity. We have the best-equipped, most high-tech churches imaginable to build us up spiritually. We have an educational system that, despite its flaws, is the envy of every country where Plant With

Purpose works. We have unprecedented power to travel, to give, and to make our opinions heard. We are some of the most privileged people in history. And for those to whom much is given, much will be required.

However, we are not immune to the same lie that the poor confront—the lie that we have nothing to offer, that our contribution is unimportant. This idea is pervasive in our own society. Even as I write this, I struggle to fight this lie in my own life. Exposing the lie that we have nothing to offer is a fundamental part of the gospel. Part of the good news is that we all have something to contribute.

But there is also a second lie we must overcome. Just as we must get beyond the idea that we have nothing to offer, we must also set aside the belief that it's all up to us. God doesn't need us to redeem the world. That has already been done. He doesn't need us to feed the poor, or fight injustice, or rescue the planet. Rather, God *allows* us to participate with him in what he is doing in the world.

My children sometimes ask if they can help me with something I could do more easily myself. Yet I've learned that letting them help is one of the most important things I can do. God lets us help, too, not because God needs us, but because it is good for us. By participating we better understand the heart of God.

As we serve the poor, we feel God's passion for the lost and the oppressed, the widow and the orphan. We feel God's anger at injustice as we fight human trafficking. We feel God's love for the things God has created—the mountains, the forests, the streams, the creatures, and the people—as we work to protect them and serve them.

In the movie *Rudy,* the title character dreams of playing football for Notre Dame. Rudy doesn't have the size or the talent for it, but his dedication and heart earn him a spot on the team—or at least a spot on the bench. Finally, in the last game, when the outcome is assured, the coach lets Rudy play, and he plays his heart out.

That's where we are at this time in history. The outcome is assured. It may not feel like it, but the good guys are going to win.

Creation Care Has to Be Fun

It's easy for our ethic of caring for creation and our stewardship mandate to feel like drudgery. It's also easy to fall into the trap of judgmentalism and self-righteousness once we start down the road to obedient stewardship. Already, to many people, the Christian life seems like a long list of dos and don'ts (mostly don'ts).

Our family tries to cultivate a sense of adventure about connecting to creation. We remind ourselves that it doesn't take much brainpower to spend money and burn fossil fuels as we go through life. Anyone can do that. Having fun for free and making the most of what we already have takes creativity, puzzle-solving skills, and teamwork. We compost our kitchen scraps, hang out our clothes to dry, and make our own cards and presents for the same reason we watch birds and go fishing: it's fun!

The empire of consumerism and materialism makes a virtue of envy, and instructs us to sacrifice time with God and time with family to acquire stuff. When we keep the Sabbath, play games, tell stories, give stuff away, help our neighbors, dig in the garden, and make up nonsense rhymes, our family is engaged in active resistance—in powerful, joyful protest to the systems that want our conformity.

For the Christian, environmental stewardship should be marked by the same attitude as financial stewardship. In 2 Corinthians 9:7, Paul tells us to give "not reluctantly or under compulsion, for God loves a cheerful giver." The Greek word for *cheerful* has the same root as the word *hilarity*—a word that signifies joyous spontaneity. How much more generous would our service to God, our neighbors, and creation be if hilarity, rather than reluctance or compulsion, was its hallmark?

Rusty Pritchard is president and cofounder of Flourish, a collaborative ministry that helps churches care for creation in ways that honor God and help people.

Creation will be redeemed. Nonetheless, we get to be in the game! We get to participate in God's plan of redemption, announcing that his kingdom is near.

I have to remind myself of this when I'm confronted by the disparity between our tiny efforts at reforestation and the overwhelming environmental degradation that dooms so many people to hunger, poverty, and death. I am tempted to despair. Instead I must remember the privilege I have of getting to be in the game and doing what God has called me to do, participating in God's victory.

I've talked about how the call to be a hero helped catalyze my vocational shift, capturing my imagination and waking me to a wider world . . . which was good. But I have since come to realize that it is the wrong call. God has not asked us to be the heroes of the story.

My only experience at farming was a disaster. My farming career abruptly ended the day I nearly destroyed a tractor and set a field on fire, so it was foolish for me to think I could teach an African farmer how to farm. I am not the savior. Jesus is the Savior. He is not calling us to save the world; that has already been done. But he is letting us participate.

Our role is more like the role of Horton the elephant in the Dr. Seuss book *Horton Hears a Who*. Horton hears a community of tiny people who live on an insignificant dust speck. No one else can hear them, and it is up to him to ensure that the people are not destroyed. His job is to tell a callous world there are people living there. But ultimately it is up to the people of Whoville to act. And it is the smallest Who—"the least of these"—who comes closest to being the hero, as his little voice breaks through to the rest of the world.

Similarly, we aren't able to save the rural poor, nor can we speak for them. Our job is to ensure that their voices are heard.

It was a humbling moment when I realized that my own talents were best utilized at home in the United States, telling the story of the communities we serve, rather than in the field, rescuing people. Any of us can become aware of the poor and their reality, and then tell their story, or learn about creation and tell its story. Become a Horton. It is a more important task than you can imagine.

Once we have overcome the lie that we have nothing to offer, as well as repudiating the lie that it is all up to us, we are free to give what we do have. Our five loaves and two fish are necessary for the miracle to begin.

Globally

We Christians in the United States have an unprecedented opportunity to effect global change. We can create organizations and initiatives to bring the good news to the poor and suffering. A startling number of people are doing just that. My one word of caution is to do it wisely, learning from the mistakes of other organizations that have gone before.

We can also support the existing efforts of groups that serve the poor and creation such as Plant With Purpose, World Vision, Food for the Hungry, Care of Creation, and others. Increasingly, the work of international aid agencies includes environmental concerns. I recommend supporting agencies with long-term, ongoing development programs that empower local people, as opposed to the kind of aid that provides food, materials, or short-term projects. Look for upstream thinking.

Some of the largest secular environmental agencies are doing excellent work in linking the concerns of the poor and environmental issues, realizing that the two are intimately connected. I have visited some outstanding programs supported by WWF, and I have confidence in the work that Conservation International is doing in this area, although neither of these agencies includes an overtly spiritual dimension in their programs.

We also have the option to offer our own time and energy in areas of need. Short-term missions have grown tremendously in recent decades, and the number-one request Plant With Purpose gets from churches is for trips. While I wholeheartedly support this desire to get involved and make a difference, I have mixed feelings about mission trips. Most of the benefit accrues to the people who go on the trips, rather than the receiving communities.

Mission trips often reinforce the dependency of the local community, while building a hero complex in those who come. Still, there is no better way for Americans to get a taste of what it means to be a global Christian and develop a heart for the world than a short-term mission trip.

If we approach these trips with humility and realize we will not transform the lives of the poor with a one-week visit, they can be very valuable. The most important thing we can do is develop relationships with those who receive us.

One of the greatest gifts we can give the poor is simply to acknowledge their humanity. A Haitian farmer once told me, "We are forgotten by everyone. Even our own countrymen ignore us. So when you come here, it reminds us that we are important. That we are not totally abandoned, but that someone somewhere is praying for us and cares about us. It gives us the courage to carry on."

The next best thing visitors can do happens after they return home, when they share what they have learned with their churches and families. This task is supremely important. It requires humility, because our part in the story is diminished. We have to acknowledge that our trip did not save the poor. However, much of the injustice that happens in the world occurs because people are unseen and their stories are unknown. Injustice flourishes in the darkness. Bringing those stories to light is critical. Be a Horton.

Locally

Getting to know the natural world that surrounds us in our own backyards is also important. As Steven Bouma-Prediger points out, we can only love what we know.[3] We have become detached from the creation around us. The natural world is forgotten, and its story remains unknown. Most of us are aware of only a fraction of what we've been given in creation, so go outside, study it, learn about God from it, and share it. Turn off the TV or computer, spend more time with your family, and go for a walk.

For me this has been one of the greatest blessings of my work. I was an avid backpacker in high school and college, but during my years in the Navy, I somehow forgot the outdoors. Thanks to being around people who love creation, this passion has been returned to me. I have become an ardent, if amateur, birder and have rediscovered the beauty and wonder of the place I live. I have also realized how little I know about it.

By learning a little about creation, we can learn a lot about God. The world we've been charged to care for has a stupendous diversity of plants and creatures. The Genesis creation account tells us how God feels about his creation: it is very good.

When I was young, my father had a friend who was a magnificent craftsman, making models, furniture, and tools out of wood. I didn't know much about woodworking, but it was intuitively obvious to me that if I wanted to be this man's friend and enjoy being around him, I would need to learn more about woodworking so I could appreciate who he was as a person. We can learn a lot about God in the same way.

We can also change our own lifestyles, becoming better stewards of the earth. There are many simple ways we can do this; for example, changing standard light bulbs to compact fluorescents, installing power strips (and turning them off), buying less, shutting off the water while we soap up in the shower, line-drying our clothes. Insulate your house better and then turn down your thermostat. Drive less and ride your bike.

Taking reusable shopping bags to the market with you can be a wonderful witness. Dozens of conversations have been sparked when my fellow church members have gone to the grocery store with their "creation care team" shopping bags. Far from being a hindrance to sharing the gospel, environmental concern opens doors and demonstrates a new side of the church.

Make it a game to see how low you can get your electric bill. Then contribute the savings to help the poor plant trees. Turning off your lights can literally save lives.

When you go for a walk, clean up the trash you see. Better yet, volunteer with a local park clean-up crew, trail-building team, or habitat restoration team. You'll build new relationships as you care for God's creation.

At the Plant With Purpose office, we replaced paper towels with hand towels and eliminated paper plates and disposable silverware.

We save hundreds of dollars by printing on scratch paper. Lately we have been testing our limits with worm-composting bins in the staff bathroom. Nancy Sleeth's book, *Go Green, Save Green,* provides an exhaustive list of ways we can not only be better stewards, but save money as well.[4]

One important step is to change our habits in what we eat and the way we eat. Reducing the meat we consume, and eating seafood only from sustainable fisheries are two easy actions. Monterey Bay Aquarium's Seafood Watch Guide, available online, can help simplify seafood decisions.[5]

Many of the agricultural techniques Plant With Purpose uses, techniques that mimic the cycles of creation, are applicable to the way we farm in the United States. You can support the efforts of those who use them by buying locally grown food or becoming a member of a community-supported agriculture association.

Another way you can help is to grow your own food. This is very much in vogue these days, and it is a great way to reconnect to the earth. With the current economic downturn, gardening has become popular. Even the White House has a vegetable garden. It may seem a tiny gesture, but it serves several functions. By growing some of your own food, we can begin to break free of the industrial food chain that is the source of so many of our environmental and health problems. Digging in the soil reconnects us with creation. It will also help us better understand the life of subsistence farmers, who have only what they plant to live on.

Start small. My parents had a garden for a year or two while I was growing up. It seemed like a lot of work, and for a short time each year we had way too many zucchinis. However, at an agricultural missions conference hosted by the Christian agency ECHO a few years ago, I saw a presentation by the originator of the Square Foot Garden system,[6] which focused on planting small amounts of a diversity of vegetables, rotating them, and staggering the planting, so you always have a useable variety.

My first step was to replace what I was buying at the supermarket with what I could grow at home. I quickly learned, though, that I could grow all kinds of things that weren't even available at the supermarket. That was when I discovered heirloom seeds:

thousands of varieties of tomatoes, peppers, lettuce, carrots, and corn—another reminder of the diversity of creation.

Commercially available produce is not necessarily bred for taste or nutrition. As a result, we miss out on all sorts of things without even knowing it. Becoming a good steward is not necessarily a path toward hardship and privation. It can bring a great deal of richness to our lives.

Rusty Pritchard once suggested to me that a first step toward caring for the creation might be simply to put up a bird feeder. A tiny, easy step, but one that sets the tone: enjoying creation, becoming more aware of our local environment, and learning to love our corner of it.

You can also be a catalyst for creation care at your local church. Start a recycling program. Conduct an energy audit. Plant a garden and serve the needy from it. If you don't have a creation-care committee, stewardship committee, or green team, talk to your pastor about starting one. Ask your pastor to preach on the topic of creation care.

Your initial steps can be as simple as the beach clean-up that our church did, or as complex as Solana Beach Presbyterian Church's community-service day, in which nearly two thousand people deployed into the community, doing everything from cleaning up trash to clearing invasive species and replanting native species in the local lagoon. Contact Plant With Purpose or visit www.PlantWithPurpose.org for additional ideas on greening your church.

These are baby steps. Five loaves and two fish. But they're a great place to start.

As the list of ways we might care for the earth gets longer, the danger is that creation care may become burdensome or onerous. I was recently asked, "How much is enough? If I change all my light bulbs to compact fluorescents, is that enough?"

But I believe that question gets us headed down the wrong track. It reminds me of the rich young man who asked Jesus if what he was doing was enough for salvation. "I have followed all of the commandments," he said. "What else do I have to do?" Jesus told him to sell all his possessions and give the money to the poor. (See Matthew 19:21.) I don't think Jesus answered in this way because he wants all of us to sell our possessions, but because it was the one area this young man was not willing to give over.

When we ask, "What else must I do?" the answer is always "The next thing." We are called to take the next step—but only the next step. One at a time. I have only begun to take the first steps. They have been far less painful than I expected. Lord willing, I will be able to take more steps toward being a good steward. How much is enough? There is no "enough."

The task can be pretty daunting, and it is easy to be driven by guilt. Like the Pharisees, we can find ourselves tithing cumin and dill, and expecting others to do the same, all the while missing the big point. Our friends won't want to be around us if we become eco-legalists. The grace of God, which says we are saved by faith and not by works, frees us to respond out of gratitude and joy rather than guilt.

Our response should never be a guilt-driven laundry list of lifestyle changes and things to feel bad about. We should not approach our call to stop sinning, or to prayer, or to share the good news, or to do justice out of guilt either. Like all of these, our care for the creation should be driven by a desire to love others because God first loved us.

Whatever steps we take, we can be certain our labor will not be in vain. Jesus loves his creation and has a plan to redeem it. And we have been given a role to play in that redemption. So let's get in the game.

Notes

Introduction

1. Bob Shacochis, *The Immaculate Invasion* (New York: Penguin Books, 1999), 270.

Chapter 1

1. Anup Shah, "Poverty Facts and Stats," Global Issues: Social, Political, Economic, and Environmental Issues That Affect Us All, www.globalissues.org/article/26/poverty-facts-and-stats#src1 (accessed July 7, 2009).

2. Susan Llewelyn Leach, "Slavery Is Not Dead, Just Less Recognizable," *Christian Science Monitor,* September 1, 2004, www.csmonitor.com/2004/0901/p16s01-wogi.html (accessed April 20, 2009).

Chapter 2

1. "The State of Food Insecurity in the World, 2005," Food and Agriculture Organization of the United Nations, (Rome: Food and Agriculture Organization of the United Nations, 2005) 24. This publication is also available online at ftp://ftp.fao.org/docrep/fao/008/a0200e/a0200e.pdf

2. "Rural Poverty Report 2001: The Challenge of Ending Rural Poverty," International Fund for Agricultural Development, (Oxford: Oxford University Press, 2001), 36. This publication is also available online at www.ifad.org/poverty/

3. Obviously it is difficult and somewhat presumptuous to describe the lifestyle of one billion people in uniform generalities. The situations vary considerably from country to country and even household to household. The example here is a hybrid of several countries, most closely resembling rural Haiti, and is included to give a general impression of the people we are discussing.

4. Rhett A. Butler, "Deforestation in the Amazon," www.mongabay
.com/brazil.html (accessed July 3, 2009).

5. "Threats from Humankind," http://rainforests.mongabay.com/
0803.htm (accessed July 3, 2009).

6. "The Challenge of Rural Energy Poverty in Developing Countries,"
Appendix: FAO Data on Woodfuels (1995 figures), World Energy Council.

7. "2007/2008 Human Development Report: 23 Energy Sources,"
http://hdrstats.undp.org/en/indicators/228.html (accessed June 15, 2009).

8. Susan C. Stonich and Billie R. DeWalt, "The Political Ecology of
Deforestation in Honduras," in *Tropical Deforestation: The Human
Dimension*, ed. Leslie E. Sponsel, Thomas N. Headland, and Robert C.
Bailey (New York: Columbia University Press, 1996), 187.

9. Paul W. Brand, "A Handful of Mud: A Personal History of My Love
for the Soil," in *Tending the Garden: Essays on the Gospel and the Earth*,
ed. Wesley Granberg-Michaelson (Grand Rapids: Eerdmans, 1987),
136–150.

10. Ibid.

11. David Pimentel, "Soil Erosion: A Food and Environmental
Threat," *Environment, Development and Sustainability*, vol. 8 (2006),
119–187.

12. Pimentel, 123.

13. Ibid.

14. Chris C. Park, *Tropical Rainforests* (London: Routledge, 1992), 97.

15. University of Washington. "The Woes of Kilimanjaro: Don't Blame
Global Warming," *ScienceDaily*, June 12, 2007, www.sciencedaily
.com/releases/2007/06/070611153942.htm (accessed July 27, 2009).

16. Bettwy, Mike. "Tropical Deforestation Affects Rainfall in the U.S.
and Around the Globe," www.nasa.gov/centers/goddard/news/topstory/
2005/deforest_rainfall.html (accessed May 27, 2009).

17. William G. Deutsh, et al., "Community-Based Water Quality Monitoring," in *Seeking Sustainability: Challenges of Agricultural Development and Environmental Management in a Philippine Watershed*, Ian
Coxhead and Gladys Buenavista, eds. (Los Baños, Laguna: Philippine
Council for Agriculture, Forestry and Natural Resources Research and
Development, 2001), 138–154.

18. *Ecosystem Services: A Primer*, from the Ecological Society of America, available at www.actionbioscience.org/environment/esa.html (accessed
February 26, 2009).

19. UNICEF United States Fund, "Water and Sanitation for All: Bringing the Issue Home," http://youth.unicefusa.org/assets/pdf/water_elementary_final.pdf (accessed July 8, 2009).

20. John Manuel, Erin E. Dooley, "The Quest for Fire: Hazards of a Daily Struggle," in *Environmental Health Perspectives*, January 2003, A33.

21. Luisa Massarani and Mike Shanahan, "Amazon Studies Link Malaria to Deforestation," *Science and Development Network*, www.scidev.net/News/index.cfm?fuseaction=readNews&itemid=2627&language=1 (accessed February 26, 2006).

22. David Taylor, "Seeing the Forest for More than the Trees," in *Environmental Health Perspectives*, November 1997, 1186–91.

Chapter 3

1. Myers, Bryant L., *Walking with the Poor: Principles and Practices of Transformational Development* (Maryknoll: Orbis Books, 1999), 115–117.

Chapter 4

1. P. K. Ramachandran Nair, *An Introduction to Agroforestry* (Dordrecht: Kluwer Academic Publishers, 1993), 43–45.

2. Don Brandt, ed., *Inheriting the Earth: Poor Communities and Environmental Renewal* (Monrovia: World Vision Resources, 2004).

3. Joe Muwonge and Don Brandt, "Food Security and Environmental Renewal through Agroforestry," in *Inheriting the Earth: Poor Communities and Environmental Renewal*, ed. Don Brandt (Monrovia: World Vision Resources, 2004), 51–71.

4. This has been an ongoing process, and our program team has done some wonderful work in reorienting our thinking to outcomes as opposed to activities.

5. David Evans, "Redemptive Agriculture: Working the Land that God Entrusted to Us" (unpublished Bible study curriculum, *Food for the Hungry*, given to the author 2006).

6. Corey Flintoff, "In Haiti a Low-Wage Job Is Better than None," *All Things Considered*, National Public Radio, June 14, 2009, www.npr.org/templates/story/story.php?storyId=104403034.

7. Michael P. Todaro and Stephen C. Smith, *Economic Development: Ninth Edition* (New York: Pearson Addison Wesley, 2005), 344.

8. "Farming God's Way," www.farming-gods-way.org (accessed July 7, 2009).

9. ECHO (www.echonet.org) offers strongly recommended resources for churches or individuals who are interested in incorporating agriculture into an overseas outreach or mission program. Much of their materials can also be used to improve gardening and in small-scale agriculture in the United States.

10. Michael Pollan, "The Food Issue: An Open Letter to the Next Farmer in Chief," *New York Times,* October 12, 2008, www.ny times.com/2008/10/12/magazine/12policy-t.html (accessed February 28, 2009).

11. Roland Bunch, *Two Ears of Corn: A Guide to People-Centered Agricultural Improvement* (Oklahoma City: World Neighbors, 1995), 138.

12. Tony Rinaudo, "The Environment: Cross Cutting Issue or Cornerstone?" in *Inheriting the Earth: Poor Communities and Environmental Renewal,* ed. Don Brandt (Monrovia: World Vision Resources, 2004), 27.

Chapter 5

1. Kiva, "Loans that Change Lives," www.kiva.org.

2. Jared Diamond, *Collapse: How Societies Choose to Fail or Succeed* (Boston: Penguin Books, 2005), 352.

3. Bunch, 128.

4. Rajdeep Sengupta and Craig P. Aubuchon, "The Microfinance Revolution: An Overview," *Federal Reserve Bank of St. Louis Review,* January/February 2008, 20.

5. Susan Johnson and Ben Rogaly, *Microfinance and Poverty Reduction: Oxfam Development Guidelines* (London: Oxfam Publishing, 1997), 8.

6. Ibid.

7. William J. Grant and Hugh C. Allen, "CARE's Mata Masu Dubara (MMD) Program in Niger: Successful Financial Intermediation in the Rural Sahel," *Journal of Microfinance,* Vol. 4 (2), Fall 2002, 189–216.

8. Johnson and Rogaly, 20–21.

9. Lennart Båge, "Microfinance: Macro Benefits, Savings—The Forgotten Half of Microfinance," International Fund for Agricultural Development, www.ifad.org/events/microcredit/op.htm (accessed May 17, 2009).

Chapter 6

1. Human Rights Watch, "'Illegal People': Haitians and Dominico-Haitians in the Dominican Republic," April 4, 2002, B1401, www.unhcr .org/refworld/docid/3cf2429a4.html (accessed July 28, 2009).

2. Jeffery Gettleman, "Albinos in Tanzania Face Deadly Threat," *The New York Times,* June 8, 2008, www.nytimes.com/2008/06/08/world/africa/08iht-tanzania.1.13549207.html (accessed July 8, 2009).

3. Diamond, 320–328.

4. Bryant L. Myers, *Walking with the Poor: Principles and Practices of Transformational Development* (Maryknoll: Orbis Books, 1999), 207.

5. Ibid, 111–112.

6. J. J. Kritzinger, "The Rwandan Tragedy as Public Indictment of Christian Mission," *Missionalia* 24:3, 1996, www.geocities.com/missionalia/rwanda1.htm (accessed June 15, 2009).

Chapter 7

1. Banff-Bow Valley Task Force, Canada, *Banff-Bow Valley at the Crossroads* (Banff National Park: Banff, Alta, 1996).

2. Anis Rahman, Ian Popay, and Trevor James, "Invasive Plants in Agro-Ecosystems in New Zealand: Environmental Impact and Risk Assessment," *Food & Fertilizer Technology Center for the Asian and Pacific Region,* www.agnet.org/library/eb/539 (accessed June 30, 2009).

3. Neville Peat, *Land Aspiring: The Story of Mount Aspiring National Park* (Nelson: Craig Potton Publishing, 1994), 70–73.

4. Diamond, 425–426.

5. Daniel Pauly, "Anecdotes and the Shifting Baseline Syndrome of Fisheries," *Trends in Ecology and Evolution* 10(10):430, 1995.

6. J. B. C. Jackson, "Reefs Since Columbus," *Coral Reefs,* 16 (1997), Suppl.: S23–S32.

7. C. S. Lewis, *Poems,* ed. Walter Hooper (San Diego: Harcourt, Inc., 1977), 61.

8. Matthew Sleeth, "Introduction: The Power of a Green God," *The Green Bible* (New York: HarperCollins Publishers, 2008), I-17.

9. Report of the Secretary-General, "Reversing the Loss of Forest Cover, Preventing Forest Degradation in All Types of Forests and Combating Desertification, Including in Low Forest Cover Countries," United Nations Forum on Forests, eighth session (New York, 20 April–1 May 2009), 5.

10. Diamond, 487.

11. IPCC Fourth Assessment Report, Working Group I Report, "The Physical Science Basis," Section 7.3.3.1.5, 527.

12. Azadeh Ansari, "Global Warming Threatens Forests, Study Says," CNN.com Breaking News, www.cnn.com/2009/TECH/science/01/22/study.forests.dying/index.html (accessed April 13, 2009).

13. University of California–Santa Barbara, "Earth in Midst of Sixth Mass Extinction: 50% of All Species Disappearing." *ScienceDaily,* October 21, 2008, www.sciencedaily.com /releases/2008/10/081020171454 .htm (accessed April 29, 2009).

14. Bryan Walsh, "Saving Species in the New Age of Extinction," *Time,* April 13, 2009, 46.

15. Millennium Ecosystem Assessment, *Ecosystems and Human Wellbeing: Synthesis* (Washington, DC: Island Press, 2005).

16. Abraham McLaughlin and Christian Allen Purefoy, "Hunger is spreading in Africa," *Christian Science Monitor,* August 1, 2005.

17. "Secretary-General, in message for day to combat desertification and drought, stresses need to reconsider agricultural practices, water management," United Nations press release, June 11, 2009, www.un.org/ News/Press/docs/2009/sgsm12304.doc.htm (accessed June 20, 2009).

18. "The Rise and Fall of Atlantic Cod," *Canadian Geographic,* www.canadiangeographic.ca/specialfeatures/atlanticcod/codhome.asp (accessed June 25, 2009).

19. "Big-Fish Stocks Fall 90 Percent Since 1950, Study Says," *National Geographic News,* May 15, 2003, http://news.nationalgeographic.com/ news/2003/05/0515_030515_fishdecline.html (accessed April 30, 2009).

20. Richard Black, "'Only 50 Years Left' for Sea Fish," BBC News, November 2, 2006, http://news.bbc.co.uk/2/hi/science/nature/6108414 .stm (accessed April 30, 2009).

21. Scott LaFee, "Fish Story: Novel Study Shows Trophy Reef Catch Reduced to Small Fry," *San Diego Union-Tribune,* March 9, 2009.

22. Black.

23. "Solving the Mystery of the Coral Triangle," CRC Reef Research Centre Ltd., http://www.reef.crc.org.au/publications/newsletter/june04 _coraltriangle.htm (accessed June 27, 2009).

24. Clive Wilkinson, ed., *Status of Coral Reefs of the World: 2004* (Global Coral Reef Monitoring Network), 7.

25. C. J. Moore, G. L. Lattin, and A. F. Zellers, "Density of Plastic Particles Found in Zooplankton Trawls from Coastal Waters of California to the North Pacific Central Gyre," Algalita Marine Research Foundation, http://alguita.com/pdf/Density-of-Particles.pdf (accessed July 13, 2009).

26. J. Matthew Sleeth, *Serve God, Save the Planet: A Christian Call to Action* (Grand Rapids: Zondervan, 2006), 28.

27. Dr. Kristen Kerksiek, "Dying for Clean Water," *Infection Research,* May 19, 2009, www.infection-research.de/perspectives/

detail/pressrelease/clean_water_a_medical_breakthrough (accessed May 30, 2009).

28. Fourth Assessment Report, Intergovernmental Panel on Climate Change (IPCC), www.ipcc.ch.

Chapter 8

1. Leroy Barber, "Green My Hood" (presentation at Flourish 2009 Conference, Duluth, GA, May 13–15, 2009).

2. Paul Mohai and Robin Saha, "Racial Inequality in the Distribution of Hazardous Waste: A National-Level Reassessment," *Social Problems,* vol. 54, issue 3 (August 2007), 343–370.

3. Robert D. Bullard, "Environmental Justice in the 21st Century: Race Still Matters," *Phylon (1960–),* vol. 49, no. 3/4 (Autumn–Winter 2001), 151–171.

4. Aliyah Baruchin, "For Minority Kids, No Room to Breathe," *The New York Times,* August 30, 2007, http://health.nytimes.com/ref/health/healthguide/esn-asthmachildren-ess.html (accessed July 8, 2009).

5. Dina Cappiello, "Air Has Elevated Cancer Risk in 600 Neighborhoods," *Chicago Tribune,* June 24, 2009, http://archives.chicagotribune.com/2009/jun/24/news/chi-ap-us-airtoxics (accessed June 30, 2009).

6. "Understanding New National Data on Lead Poisoning," Alliance for Healthy Homes, www.afhh.org/chil_ar/chil_ar_lead_poisoning_BLL_data_factsheet.htm (accessed June 1, 2009).

7. "Learn More about Mountaintop Removal Coal Mining," *End Mountaintop Removal Action and Resource Center,* www.ilovemountains.org/resources (accessed May 15, 2009).

8. Christians for the Mountains, www.christiansforthemountains.org.

9. Jason DinAlt, "The Environmental Impact of Immigration into the United States," reprinted from Carrying Capacity Network's Focus, vol. 4, no. 2, 1997, www.carryingcapacity.org/DinAlt.htm (accessed June 15, 2009).

10. Joel Simon, *Endangered Mexico: An Environment on the Edge* (San Francisco: Sierra Club Books, 1997), 35.

11. Ibid.

12. Norman Myers, "Environmental Refugees: A Growing Phenomenon of the 21st Century," *Philosophical Transactions: Biological Sciences,* vol. 357, no. 1420, Reviews and a Special Collection of Papers on Human Migration (April 29, 2002), 609–613.

13. Susan Llewelyn Leach, "Slavery Is Not Dead, Just Less Recognizable," *Christian Science Monitor,* September 1, 2004, www.csmonitor.com/2004/0901/p16s01-wogi.html (accessed April 20, 2009).

Chapter 9

1. Tony Campolo, *How to Rescue the Earth Without Worshiping Nature* (Nashville: Thomas Nelson Publishers, 1992), 13.

2. Gary W. Fick, *Food, Farming, and Faith* (Albany: State University of New York, 2008), 19.

3. Steven Bouma-Prediger, *For the Beauty of the Earth: A Christian Vision for Creation Care* (Grand Rapids: Baker Academic, 2001), 76–77.

4. Vernon J. Bourke, ed., *Essential Augustine* (Boston: Hackett Company, 1974), 123.

5. Bouma-Prediger, 13.

6. John Wesley, Charles Bonnet, and Louis Dutens, *A Survey of the Wisdom of God in the Creation,* 3rd ed. (New York: Bangs and Mason, 1823), 8.

7. Stephen Tomkins, *William Wilberforce: A Biography* (Oxford: Lion, 2007), 207.

8. Basil Miller, *William Carey: The Father of Modern Missions* (Minneapolis: Bethany House Publishers, 1985).

9. Vishal and Ruth Mangalwadi, *The Legacy of William Carey: A Model for the Transformation of a Culture* (Wheaton: Crossway Books, 1999), 22.

10. Ibid, 19.

11. Darrow Miller, "Agriculture and the Kingdom of God," in *Biblical Holism and Agriculture,* eds. David J. Evans, Ronald J. Vos, and Keith P. Wright (Pasadena: William Carey Library, 2003), 157.

12. Vineyard Boise Online, www.vineyardboise.org/Ministries/Barnabas.aspx.

13. Catherine Bertini and Dan Glickman, "Farm Futures: Bringing Agriculture Back to U.S. Foreign Policy," *Foreign Affairs,* vol. 88, no. 3, May/June 2009, 97.

14. Diamond, 344.

Chapter 10

1. Anup Shah, "Poverty Facts and Stats," *Global Issues: Social, Political, Economic, and Environmental Issues that Affect Us All,* www.globalissues.org/article/26/poverty-facts-and-stats#src1 (accessed July 7, 2009).

2. Van Jones, *The Green Collar Economy: How One Solution Can Fix Our Two Biggest Problems* (New York: HarperCollins Publishers, 2008).

3. Bouma-Prediger, 37.

4. Nancy Sleeth, *Go Green, Save Green: A Simple Guide to Saving Time, Money, and God's Green Earth* (Carol Stream: Tyndale House, 2009).

5. "Seafood Watch," Monterrey Bay Aquarium, www.montereybay aquarium.org/cr/seafoodwatch.aspx.

6. Mel Bartholomew, *Square Foot Gardening* (Emmaus: Rodale Press, 1981). See also www.squarefootgardening.com.

Creation Care
A Small Group Study Guide

By Scott C. Sabin and Rebecca Buckham

Using This Study

Before giving you some helpful tips on how to use this study, we would like to give you an idea of why Plant With Purpose has taken the time to put together a resource for individuals and churches interested in learning more about caring for creation.

Founded in 1984, Plant With Purpose is a Christian nonprofit organization that works to reverse deforestation and poverty in the world by transforming the lives of the rural poor. Plant With Purpose began work in the Dominican Republic and has since established economic development programs in rural communities in the Caribbean, Latin America, Africa, and Asia. Based on the acknowledgment that poverty is intimately connected with environmental degradation, Plant With Purpose's programs work to reverse these problems simultaneously by addressing their root causes and modeling alternative methods of generating income and using land. This involves community development that encourages poor farmers to take ownership of problems and work toward solutions; innovative agriculture and forestry that enables communities to use resources in a sustainable manner; microenterprise that contributes to a village's economic diversification; and discipleship that shares the good news of Jesus Christ and helps people become servant leaders in their communities.

More than anything, it is our hope that this study will encourage discussion about a Christian response to the issue of environmental health. The Introduction establishes environmental stewardship as an ethic of care for creation and identifies four relationships around which this study is organized: we might call these the relationships of stewardship.

Chapters 1 through 4 address these four relationships. Relevant passages from the Bible (NIV translation) accompany each section of text, along with questions to prompt dialogue within a group setting. You might encourage individuals to do the readings and look up passages independently, allowing you to focus your group meeting on the discussion questions. Alternatively, you may look up and respond to the Scripture passages together. "In Action" suggestions are provided to help you enrich your group's understanding of the four relationships. The Conclusion reviews each relationship and prompts discussion on how to implement an ethic of environmental stewardship in each individual's life and in your church community.

This study guide may be easily adapted for use in a four- or six-week format, depending on whether the Introduction and Conclusion are used as separate sessions. However you use this study, we hope it is thought-provoking and challenging. We have also included an index of resources for further study and action. If you are interested in finding out more about how to support or become involved with Plant With Purpose, or if you have any suggestions that might help us improve our curriculum, please let us know. May God bless you and your church community as you learn more about relationship with this good and beautiful creation!

Introduction

Window on the World: Despite the afternoon heat, the small group of women sets out for the long daily trek to the nearest water source, a spring several miles from their rural village. These women spend much of their time collecting what their families need for drinking, cooking, and washing. Closer water sources have dried up or become dangerously contaminated because poverty has driven villagers to cut down the surrounding forests for quick cash.

These women might have once walked beneath the dense canopy of a lush tropical forest to collect water from clean rivers and streams closer to their homes. The poverty of their communities, however, makes them dependent on unsustainable land practices like slash-and-burn agriculture. As a result, the ground is hard and rocky, having lost its topsoil to the erosion that occurs without a network of tree roots to hold the soil in place. When it rains, hillsides wash away in mudslides and flash floods pollute rivers and destroy homes. For these women, and for many poor communities on our planet, daily survival depends on the land and its resources. When the land is impoverished, its people will remain in poverty.

"Green" Christians?

The hardships faced by these communities are linked to environmental health. Deforestation, pollution, famine, unsanitary water sources, and events such as drought, flooding, and mudslides are environmental issues. For Christians, who have been charged with caring for the poor, a response to poverty must include responding to the environmental issues in which poverty is rooted. How should Christians respond to environmental issues? What does Christianity have to do with the environment? Some would say "nothing." Others might go further and put an exclamation point at the end of "nothing!" in order to distance themselves from "liberal tree-huggers." Is it possible for someone to be both a Christian and an environmentalist?

Many different voices identify themselves as environmentalists. Perhaps the best definition of *environmentalist* is one who values the health of the natural world. This might be someone who enjoys hiking, camping, and fishing. This includes people who want to protect areas of land from industry and development, as well as those who want to preserve our habitat and its natural resources for future generations. This also includes more distinct groups such as animal rights activists, deep ecologists, and biocentrists. There are many reasons that someone might care about the natural world. Consequently, the environmental community is a diverse group of voices, and those voices do not always agree.

This small-group study assumes that Christianity is a voice worth hearing and that Christians have a responsibility to participate in dialogue about the environment. Our overarching goal in this study is to discover just what it is that Christians may have to say to the larger environmental community.

- What comes to mind when you hear the word *environmentalist* or *environmentalism*?
- What reservations might you (or other Christians) have about environmentalism? Where do these concerns come from?
- What kinds of ideas might other environmentalists have about Christians?
- Why might it be important for Christians to care about the environment?

The Symphony of Creation

The first thing Christians have to say to the environmental community has to do with the way we talk about the environment.

While the natural world does indeed have value as a place of recreation, as something to protect for future generations, and for its natural resources that sustain human life, these are not the only or primary reasons the environment has value. For Christians, the environment has value because God has created it and called it "good" (Genesis 1:31). This world, of which humans are an important part, is God's creation. We refer to it as "creation" because this indicates the presence of a Creator, and because it affirms that everything that exists ultimately belongs to God.

Perhaps the most important distinction to make between Christians and other environmentalists, however, is the role of God in creation. Debates regarding the origin of life often miss what is most important: regardless of how the world came to be, God is responsible for its existence and has called human beings to be stewards of it. Our concerns should be focused on how to best live on earth.

In order to get a sense of God's feeling about creation, it might be helpful to use the metaphor of creation as a symphony. In the Bible, creation is frequently described as singing or making music. The poetry of the psalms is especially rich with musical imagery that describes creation. In Psalm 98:4, for example, the psalmist addresses the earth: "Shout for joy to the Lord, all the earth, burst into jubilant song with music." The psalmist continues the metaphor: "Let the sea resound, and everything in it, the world, and all who live in it. Let the rivers clap their hands, let the mountains sing together for joy" (vv. 7-8).

Expanding on these images can give us a fuller understanding of creation's value. God has written this symphony with painstaking care, imagining how its elements will fit together, giving full attention to each instrument and how its notes will play out among the others. In the Genesis story, God also conducts the symphony, calling out to each instrument and drawing its voice into the increasingly complex work of creation. When the many instruments in a symphony interact well, they produce the harmony of sound intended by the composer and brought to life by the conductor. Similarly, God intends a harmony of relationships for creation, which the Lord both composes and conducts. In Genesis, this harmony is achieved, and God calls this symphony "very good." And throughout history, God continually enjoys the music of creation, relishing its sound and taking pride in its beauty.

Perhaps this image of creation helps to set a context for exploring our responsibility for the health of this symphony. If God loves creation in this way, shouldn't our love for God motivate us to care for the earth in order to ensure that this symphony continues to thrive and play the music God intends?

- How are you dependent on the natural world?
- What "voices" of creation do you hear where you live?
- How have you experienced the natural world as God's creation having divine value?

Rediscovering Stewardship

When we understand the value that creation has in the eyes of God, we must conclude that, yes, Christians do have something to contribute to conversations about the environment. In fact, we could even say that our faith is "environmentally friendly" with a strong ethic of care for creation. This ethic is best expressed in the model for creation care known as Christian environmental stewardship. As a model, stewardship attempts to give us a picture of reality so that we can better understand our world and our place in it. A steward is someone who represents a higher authority, such as a king, and who has been entrusted with responsibility to care for what belongs to that higher authority. In the Christian model of stewardship, God is ruler of creation and humans are stewards on earth. As Christians, we acknowledge that creation belongs ultimately to God, and so we seek to take care of creation in a way that honors and pleases God.

Unfortunately, Christians have not always succeeded in taking care of creation in a manner that honors and pleases its Creator. Stewardship has often been misinterpreted and misunderstood, and this is one reason the Christian voice has been largely absent from conversations about the environment. Many church communities have reduced the language of stewardship so that it only applies to financial resources. More often than not, a message on stewardship is followed by the passing of offering plates and an exhortation to give generously. But this giving is limited to what comes out of pockets and checkbooks. If God is to be truly sovereign over all areas of our lives, then stewardship applies to all of those same areas, including our attitudes toward and treatment of creation. Good stewardship is taking care of all that God has given to us, including the natural world and its resources.

This study seeks to rediscover the meaning of stewardship by examining four relationships integral to any discussion of Christianity and environmental issues. These relationships are those between Creator and creation, God and humanity, humanity and habitat, and human and human. In examining stewardship within the context of these four relationships, we hope to come to a fuller understanding of what it means to be a good steward of creation. Then we can confidently participate in discussions about our environment and offer a much-needed perspective on our relationship with and responsibilities toward the natural world.

- How have you heard the word *steward* or *stewardship* used?
- When have you experienced God's presence through nature? What was revealed?
- How can Christians bring a unique voice to the current conversation on the environment?

Action Steps

1. Compile a list of the areas in which you and your church community currently demonstrate stewardship. What are the strengths and weaknesses in your stewardship practices?
2. Develop a list of the ways in which your church community has interacted with your local environment. How frequent (and recent) have those interactions been? In what areas of ministry, outreach, or activity are your interactions focused?

Creator–Creation

Theme: God has forged a covenant relationship with an inherently good creation that reveals and glorifies its Creator.

Window on the World: In the distance, smoke rises from the mountains where tracts of forest are cleared for slash-and-burn agriculture. Nearer fields now struggle to produce enough food to sustain a community. God intended this earth to be a place of abundance, with all parts working together to provide for every need. Like women compelled to walk far from home to collect water, however, all of creation groans to be restored to the design of its Maker.

"In the beginning God created . . ." These familiar words open the biblical narrative in Genesis 1:1. They are an important beginning for our study, because two key things embedded in this phrase form the foundational element for a proper understanding of Christian environmental stewardship. The first three words, "In the beginning," are important because they start something. Like a theater curtain dramatically drawn aside, they draw our attention to a story—a story we know well, a story we believe is true, and a story we wish to share with others. We are talking here about our faith. Sometimes we are so familiar with our own faith story we forget how it begins, and so it is important we go back to its very first scene and imagine ourselves as viewers. As humans, we will have an important role to play, but we have not yet appeared in the Genesis account. Before we can understand our role, we must become familiar with the bigger picture—we must know our context. Once we have taken our seats and the curtain has been drawn, we can focus on the action unfolding onstage.

The second part of this opening phrase—"God created"—tells us what this story is about. It is about a relationship—a relationship between God and what God creates. From these first words of Genesis, we see that our faith story begins with a relationship between Creator and creation. This is the central relationship to an ethic of environmental stewardship, and thus an understanding of this Creator–Creation relationship is essential for Christians seeking to understand how best to care for the earth.

Creation in Relation

"God saw all that he had made, and it was very good."
(Genesis 1:31)

What exactly is a relationship? To begin our study of stewardship relationships, we should start by asking this question. Usually we think about relationship in human terms. Our most obvious relationships are those with whom we live, work, and worship: our families, coworkers, and fellow church members. We also believe that the individual must be spirituality healthy, and thus we seek relationship with Jesus Christ. Finally, we believe that the Bible calls Christians to help others enter and experience relationship with God, and so we nurture relationships with those outside of our immediate community of family and friends. Whatever the context, however, relationship always involves two: oneself and another.

Although we usually think about relationship from a human standpoint, we see in the first chapter of Genesis a different kind of relationship. In this relationship, which opens the biblical story, the self is God and the other is creation. This relationship exists before human life, so before we can begin to consider how human beings should relate to the natural world, we must understand how God relates to creation.

- Read Genesis 1:1–2:3. How does the earth participate in creation? When human society values the earth as simply "good for," how does that compare to God's value of it?
- Read Isaiah 40:12, 25-26. What stands out to you in these verses?
- Read John 1:1-3; 3:16. What is the role of Christ in creation? What does God love? What does Christ's incarnation mean for the physical, material universe?
- Read Psalm 104. How does this psalm reflect creation as God's home? What does God do to sustain creation and provide for all creatures?

God's Other Book

"The heavens declare the glory of God." (Psalm 19:1)

As any artist is known through his or her work, so our Creator God is revealed through creation. Christians refer to the person of Jesus Christ and the Bible as "special revelation." Nature is traditionally considered a complementary form of revelation, part of what is termed "general revelation." In medieval Christianity, the natural world was sometimes called "God's other book." Indeed, scientists in the early modern era believed that exploration of the natural world was an important way to learn about God. The idea that creation communicates something about God is found throughout the Bible, in passages that use nature imagery to express divine characteristics or that incorporate elements of creation in worship.

In the psalms, creation is frequently portrayed as worshipping God through its natural elements. In the New Testament, Jesus makes references to the natural world to communicate truth about God. For example, Jesus compares the kingdom of God to a mustard seed (Mark 4:30-32) and illustrates healthy spiritual relationships with the image of a vine and branches (John 15:1-8). In these and other instances, creation serves to reveal truth about God as Creator.

- Read Romans 1:20. What does creation reveal about God? What "invisible" attributes of God can we identify in the natural world?
- Read Psalms 19:1-4; 96:11-12. What verbs does the psalmist use when referring to the natural world? What does this language tell us about creation's purpose?
- Read Psalm 148. Who or what participates in praising God?

A Covenant with Creation

"I will remember my covenant between me and you and all living creatures of every kind." (Genesis 9:15)

Scripture assures us that God does not create and then abandon creation. We will explore the effects of human sin on the created world at a later point in this study, but it is important to have an understanding of God's committed relationship with creation. This initial relationship between Creator and creation will continue throughout the Bible and history, even when sin and destruction enter the story.

We have only known a world ravaged by suffering, but when God fashioned this earth, all of creation existed in peace. *Shalom,* the Hebrew word that we translate simply as "peace," has deeper meaning in its implications for relationships. Shalom is a vision of the world characterized by healthy relationships in all areas of life. This vision of shalom offers the hope that creation can be restored to its intended state—that it can once again achieve the harmony God intended, despite immense suffering. Christians can hope for this restoration of creation because we believe that God is sovereign over creation, that the world and everything in it belong to God, and that God will remain faithful to relationship with creation.

This emphasis on hope is one distinguishing characteristic of the Christian ethic of environmental stewardship. Indeed, if God has a relationship with creation apart from humans, then concerned Christians maintain hope that God will remember that covenant relationship and not allow creation to perish.

- Read Genesis 9:8-17. With whom does God establish covenant? What does God promise?
- Read Isaiah 11:6-9. This passage envisions the *shalom* that God intends for creation. What relationships are being restored in this vision? What relevance does God's promise have for us today?
- Read Psalm 65. How does God sustain creation? How might this influence a Christian response to environmental crisis?

In Action

1. Start a "Creation Journal" for your family or your group. Keep a record of what you observe where you live and worship. Having some basic field guides to animals, birds, and plants in your local habitat might be helpful in identifying and learning more about God's world. How does what you observe communicate God?

2. Compile a songbook to be used in worship. Whether your church uses traditional hymns or contemporary worship songs, your worship most likely incorporates images of creation. Meditating on these images helps us better understand creation in its relationship to God the Creator.

3. Suggest that your church participate in Creation Care Sunday each spring. Visit Evangelical Environmental Network at www.creationcare.org for ideas on how to involve your church community in intentionally celebrating the wonder of God's creation.

God—Humanity

Theme: By approaching the natural world with the servant-ruler attitude modeled by Jesus, humans accurately reflect God's image in creation.

Window on the World: The farmers of a rural community praise God for the rain that pours down on their withering fields. Farmers recognize their responsibility to humbly protect and sustain the land that the Lord has entrusted to them. In humility and faithfulness they now protect the land in stewardship and pray for the Lord's redemption of all creation.

Although God repeatedly calls the elements of creation "good" in Genesis 1, creation is not complete without humans. Like an orchestra conductor, God brings each instrument—day and night; land, sky, and sea; sun, moon, and stars; sea creatures, birds, and animals—to life in an increasingly complex and beautiful masterpiece. Pleased with how each instrument blends its notes with those of the others, God affirms each one as "good." Finally, the human voice enters creation's song: "So God created man in his own image, in the image of God he created him; male and female he created them" (Genesis 1:27). The creation of man and woman is the central movement—God's final creative act—toward which this symphony of creation moves. While God calls the many parts of this creative work "good," the Lord now surveys everything in its completed state, and calls all of creation "very good" (Genesis 1:31).

While all of creation—God's "other book"—reflects the Creator, God chose humans to bear the divine image on earth and thus distinguished us from other creatures. Within the larger context of covenant relationship with creation, God now initiates a special relationship with human beings. Because humans bear God's image and represent God's rule on earth, the Lord gives us dominion over creation and specific instructions to "fill the earth and subdue it" and "rule" over its creatures (Genesis 1:28). These instructions have often been misinterpreted as license to use natural resources without thought or care for the well being of the earth and its non-human inhabitants. Indeed, Christianity has even been accused of contributing to ecological destruction. In this way, we have not born God's image well. If we understand God's dominion as based on a relationship that affirms creation as "very good," in itself, what should human dominion look like?

In this lesson, we will examine the nature of God's dominion in an attempt to better understand what it means for humans to have dominion over creation. Because of human sin, however, this dominion is often corrupted, and so we look to the incarnate Christ as the fulfillment of God's image and perfect dominion on earth. Christ's servant-ruler attitude gives us a model for how God's dominion is best expressed in human form. Finally, we will return to the first two chapters of Genesis to look at how Adam and Eve's stewardship of Eden illustrates this servant-ruler attitude with regard to environmental ethics.

Divine Dominion

"For dominion belongs to the LORD and he rules over the nations." (Psalm 22:28)

The word *dominion* is often associated with governments or kingdoms and refers to legal power or political authority. World history textbooks are often organized by the rise and fall of governments and kingdoms. Many of the significant dates that students memorize are those of major battles that turned the tide of a war as nations struggled for power and control of global resources. Because we live in a world in which power often involves corruption, oppression, and exploitation, we need to be careful when using the language of dominion. This dominion language is present in Genesis 1 as God gives human beings authority over other creatures and instructions to "fill the earth and subdue it." Since humans are made in God's image, we need to explore the nature of God's dominion before we can address human dominion.

Throughout the Bible, God is frequently described using this language of dominion. Psalm 9:7, for example, exalts God as one who "reigns forever," having "established his throne for judgment," and Isaiah 66:1 refers to heaven as God's throne and the earth as God's footstool. In Psalm 145:13, the poet praises God as king and God's reign as an everlasting kingdom, proclaiming that the Lord's "dominion endures through all generations." God is frequently presented as the sovereign king with dominion over creation. This dominion, however, is not corrupt and does not oppress or exploit. Psalm 9 praises God's righteous judgment, and gives thanks that this king is "a refuge for the oppressed" (v. 9) who does not forget the needy (v. 18). In Psalm 145:8-9, God is described as "gracious and compassionate, slow to anger and rich in love," and good to all of creation.

By bestowing on humans the divine image, God delegated some of this sovereign authority to men and women. This great responsibility extends to all areas of life and must not be taken lightly. With regards to the natural world, this authority does not give us the right to act without concern for ecological health. Many rulers in history have used their authority in ways that are tyrannical and lead to turmoil within a kingdom or country. By giving humans authority to rule over the earth, God entrusts us with a great responsibility to work toward the overall health of creation. Yes, humans have the right to use natural resources, but we also have the responsibility to use this authority to care for creation. Unfortunately, humans have often approached the earth with a tyrannical attitude, and today's global ill health is evidence of this misuse of dominion. When we understand how God rules as ruler of creation, we better understand what human dominion on earth should look like.

- Read Psalm 8. How does kingship language refer to humans?
- Read Psalm 95:3-7. In verse 7, what metaphor for God does the psalmist use? What kind of leader is this?
- Read Revelation 17:14. What image is used to describe God? How does this compare with our concept of dominion? How does it compare with the world's idea of dominion?

Christ the Servant-King

". . . just as the Son of Man did not come to be served, but to serve. . . ." (Matthew 20:28)

Although we are made in God's image, human beings do not always bear God's image well. Throughout the Bible, the God–Humanity relationship suffers when people identify themselves with images other than that of God. It is easy for us to develop "god-complexes" and think of ourselves not as made in the image of God but rather as gods ourselves. Human sin is rooted in pride and in the desire to become greater than we are. This temptation can even manifest itself in our attempts to help others or serve the poor. Although we image God, we do so imperfectly, which results in corrupted dominion.

To fully understand how humans are intended to bear the divine image and enact God's dominion on earth, we should look to the example of Jesus Christ, God's image perfectly manifest in human form. Jesus is the fullest revelation of God's image on earth. In Christ, God is not just *represented* by human flesh, but God actually *takes on* human flesh. In doing so, Jesus models God's dominion in the context of earthly experience. What does divine dominion look like as Christ enacts God's rule on earth?

The sovereign language used to describe God continues into the New Testament. The Bible identifies Jesus as "the image of the invisible God, the firstborn over all creation" (Colossians 1:15) and affirms Christ's sovereignty over all human kingdoms. Although the Roman soldiers in the Gospels intend to mock Jesus by placing a sign labeled "King of the Jews" above his crown of thorns, they rightly identify Christ as king even at his human death. The contrast of these two depictions—of Christ as king of creation and Christ as king on a cross—highlights what is fundamentally different about God's dominion. Jesus as servant-king has dominion that is based not on the desire for power, but on love. Out of love, Christ the servant-king refuses human power, and instead offers himself in service to others. If humans are made in the image of God, this kind of servant leadership should inform all areas of life, including our relationship with the natural world.

- Read Philippians 2:3-11. According to Paul, how did Christ use his kingly dominion? Using Jesus as a model, how should we act in areas where we have dominion?
- Read Matthew 4:1-11. How does Jesus respond when tempted with earthly dominion? What is Satan's idea of power versus God's idea of power?
- Read Mark 10:41-45. How does Jesus redefine authority?

Stewards of the Garden

"The LORD God took the man and put him in the Garden of Eden to work it and take care of it." (Genesis 2:15)

If we return to the first two chapters of Genesis, we see this kind of servant love illustrated in Adam and Eve's role as stewards in Eden. Thus far, we have focused primarily on Genesis 1 and the language of dominion in an attempt to better understand what it means for humans to bear God's image. A complete understanding of human dominion, however, must also incorporate the language of Genesis 2. While Genesis 1 gives us the big picture concerning creation and presents us with God's royal majesty and humanity's role as divinely appointed rulers, the second chapter zooms in on the first human couple and their life in Eden. Genesis 2 emphasizes God's intimate relationship with creation. While God is sovereign over creation, the Lord is also present within creation, forming a man from the earth, planting a garden, and placing Adam in Eden.

The relationship between humanity and the earth is just as

intimate: God puts humans in the garden "to work it and take care of it" (Genesis 2:15). In the Hebrew, the verbs describing Adam and Eve's role in Eden are *serve* and *protect*. In taking a look at the first two chapters of Genesis, we see that stewardship involves a balance between sovereign dominion and humble servanthood. Chapter 1 establishes human dominion, and chapter 2 illustrates how that dominion appears on a day-to-day basis. A proper understanding of dominion acknowledges that both views are necessary for a balanced perspective on Christian environmental ethics.

- Read Genesis 1:26-30; 2:15. What does an environmental ethic based on both rule and service look like?
- In what ways do humans *rule* over creation? In what ways should humans *serve* creation?

In Action

1. Throughout the week, take note of how many images. Corporate symbols, brand names, idealized faces and figures—these are all examples of images. What images dominate contemporary culture? What messages are these images communicating? How are we to think of our human identities in response to these images? Does our culture want us to believe that we are gods or that we are servants?
2. Brainstorm ideas about how you, your family, or your church community can embrace alternative images. What symbols or slogans would you choose to identify yourselves as God's image bearers? How can you communicate to others that you are a follower of Christ and not a slave to culture?
3. How does your church model stewardship? In what ways is it limited to finances? How does it extend to other areas of relationship and responsibility? How can your church community be a better servant-leader for creation? For example, conduct an audit to assess how much energy resources your building uses, or look into starting a recycling program to collect church bulletins after services.

Humanity-Habitat

Theme: Because humans are intimately connected to our earthly habitat, creation suffers in response to human sin. A Christian environmental ethic approaches the natural world with love-based humility as its defining characteristic.

Window on the World: As rural farmers are forced to walk farther each day to search for clean water, they are reminded of how utterly and fearfully dependent they are on the earth and its valuable resources. They understand that they are intrinsically linked to their environment, and must approach their habitat with an attitude of humility, instead of entitlement. Only then will their hopes of clean water and fruitful land be fulfilled.

When we hear the word *habitat*, we usually think of plants and animals before we think of people. A habitat restoration project, for example, might focus on restoring a wetland that has been dredged for commercial development. Efforts are made to vegetate the area with native species of plants in order to draw back migrating birds and provide a place for fish to spawn. The goal is to reestablish a balanced ecosystem that can support a diverse community of life forms. Human beings tend to think of ourselves as outside of such ecosystems. As we have previously explored, humans are, indeed, distinct from other forms of life in that God chose humans to represent his image most directly within Creation. Our very ability to engage in activities like habitat restoration evidences this distinction, for humans can make decisions about the natural world in a way that plants and animals cannot.

However, it is important to remember that humans, while distinct from other animals, are also creatures living in a habitat. We are dependent on the earth for sustenance—for the food that we eat, the water that we drink, and the other natural resources with which we build our lives.

But earth is more than simply a place that provides natural resources such as food, water, and shelter. The word *ecology* comes from a Greek root that translates as "house." Ecology, then, is the study of our earthly house, and ecological concerns focus on the health of this house. Recall Adam and Eve in Eden, serving and protecting their home in the garden. When we think of our habitat as also our home, will we not strive similarly to serve and protect that home? Do we not defend our homes from those who seek to destroy them?

With this understanding of habitat as home, we can further explore the Humanity–Habitat relationship we first see in Genesis 2. We will explore first how human identity is linked with the earth and how this connection is important to healthy spirituality by looking at the history of Israel and its relationship to the Promised Land. Then we will consider the consequences of human sin for creation. Finally, we will establish humility as necessary for creation's restoration, and thus as the central and defining characteristic of a Christian environmental ethic.

Humans from Humus

"The LORD God formed the man from the dust of the ground." (Genesis 2:7)

Anyone who has spread compost over a garden plot or walked through the woods during autumn knows the rich smell of humus, the decomposed organic matter of fruit peels, vegetable skins, or fallen leaves. Humus is another word for the healthy soil that results from the natural processes of death and decay. Interestingly, the words *humus* and *human* are related. Indeed, the account of Adam's creation in Genesis 2 illustrates this link between humans and soil as God forms a human being from "the dust of the ground" (v. 7), the humus of Eden. While the first human bears God's image in a way distinct from other creatures, this scene reminds us that humans are also fundamentally similar to other creatures and share much in common with our earthy habitat.

This connection with the land is not just important to human identity; it is linked to spiritual identity as well. In the Old Testament, relationship with the land is central to the God–Humanity relationship. For the Israelites, their spiritual identity as "God's chosen people" rests in the promise of healthy land, "a land flowing with milk and honey" (Exodus 3:8). The Promised Land symbolizes the covenant relationship between God and Israel, which is a relationship of blessing. Abundant land is a blessing from God, the result of Israel's righteousness.

- Read Genesis 2:7. What two elements are involved in the creation of humans? What two relationships do these represent?
- Read Deuteronomy 6:10-12; 8:6-14. What does the land promised to Israel look like? Against what does God warn in these passages?

The Land Cursed

"Cursed is the ground because of you."(Genesis 3:17)

We see the relationship between humans and habitat even more strongly when we explore the implications of human sin for creation. Throughout the Bible, creation's suffering is a direct result of human sin. This begins in Genesis, when the ground is cursed along with the serpent because of the deceived human couple (3:17), and when God resolves to cause a flood to destroy all life on the earth because of human wickedness (6:17). When Israel turns against God in disobedience to the Law, images of environmental destruction often accompany the warnings issued by Old Testament prophets. Throughout the Bible, we see that creation is highly responsive to human sin. It "vomits" out sinful people (Leviticus 18:25) and "mourns" their unfaithfulness (Hosea 4:3).

Animals, birds, and fish die in response to cursing, lying, murder, stealing, and adultery (Hosea 4:3). In the New Testament, all of creation is described as "groaning" in "bondage" as it awaits redemption (Romans 8:18-23).

What does God, the ruler of creation, have to say to humans whose sin results in destruction and interrupts the harmony of this symphony of creation? Because God seeks to defend the oppressed, part of divine justice involves judgment on those who corrupt dominion and destroy the natural world. Indeed, there will come a time not only for rewarding the righteous, but also for "destroying those who destroy the earth" (Revelation 11:18). You will recall that God, as Creator, established a covenant relationship with creation before any covenant with humankind. The Humanity–Habitat relationship may be characterized by much unfaithfulness, but the Creator will not abandon creation to destruction. Included in this covenant is punishment for those who abandon their tasks as stewards.

- Read Genesis 3:17-19. Who does God identify as responsible for creation's curse? How will humans now relate to the earth? How has their relationship with habitat changed?
- Read Isaiah 24:1-12. How is the earth affected by human sin?
- Read Ezekiel 36:1-8. To whom does the prophet speak? What does God promise?

Humility and Healed Land

"If my people, who are called by my name, will humble themselves and pray and seek my face and turn from their wicked ways, then will I hear from heaven and will forgive their sin and will heal their land." (2 Chronicles 7:14)

God invites humans to participate in creation's restoration by returning to righteousness. This is only possible if humans acknowledge God's supremacy and abandon our god complexes in pursuit of proper spiritual relationship, which must involve humility. The word *humility* also shares a common root with the words *human* and *humus*. The image of God shaping the human form *('adam)* from soil *('adamah)* is a humbling reminder that we are fundamentally made of dust, and to dust we will ultimately return. As the focus of the Christian story, Christ's incarnation emphasizes this humility, as God took on human flesh and the ruler of creation "humbled himself and became obedient to death—even death on a cross" (Philippians 2:8).

But what does Jesus' death have to do with the environment? Indeed, we typically emphasize salvation as the restoration of human relationship with God. However, the Bible makes it clear that all of creation benefits from Christ's redemptive sacrifice. John 3:16 does not limit God's love to humans, but states that God gave the Son because God "so loved the world." The Greek word translated as "world" is the same word from which we derive the English word *cosmos*—a concept that encompasses the entire planet and beyond. Similarly, Colossians 1:20 affirms that Jesus came to reconcile "all things, whether things on earth or things in heaven, by making peace through his blood, shed on the cross." What, then, should be the focus of a uniquely Christian environmental ethic? It is the presence of Christ in the Christian environmental ethic that sets our voice apart from other approaches to environmental issues because a Christian ethic models itself on the humility of its servant-king. Only by approaching creation with an attitude of humility can Christians work for the restoration of Humanity–Habitat relationship.

- Read 2 Chronicles 7:13-14. What might humility look like to you in regards to healing the earth?
- Read Psalm 37:11; Matthew 5:5. What do these Scriptures about the meek inheriting the earth mean?
- Read Mark 16:15. What might preaching the good news to all creation look like?
- Read Mark 12:28-31. If we think of our earthly habitat as our home, how can we extend love to our neighbors, both human and nonhuman?

In Action

1. To better understand the importance of soil, start a composting project at home or on your church property. Learn about the processes that break organic matter down into the humus that nourishes further life.

2. As a church, adopt a local park or road and schedule regular clean-ups that families can participate in together. Collect trash and plant trees or join a local restoration project to demonstrate a commitment to your local habitat.

3. Get involved with a community gardening project, or start your own.

4. What kinds of environmental healing would you pray for? What are the environmental issues that most impact your community? Outline ideas for how you can incorporate these into your personal and community prayer.

Human-Human

Theme: Christians follow Jesus' example and work to heal both spiritual and physical disease. Acknowledging that human suffering is often connected to unhealthy habitat, Christians work to bring the biblical hope of restoration to both people and the places in which they live.

Window on the World: Desperately attempting to survive and overcome poverty in their harsh and barren environment, rural farmers unintentionally destroy their land. But there is hope. The community is learning to work with the design of God's creation instead of against it. They recognize God's desire to restore and redeem all of creation. Because of the community's new efforts to care for and protect the environment, both the land and the people experience healing.

Within the environmental movement, the word *wilderness* is often associated with images of pristine forests, expansive mountain ranges, and untouched frontier. Accompanied by a sense of rugged individualism, this notion of wilderness emphasizes retreat from human civilization and movement toward adventure in "the great outdoors." Usually these places are characterized by healthy ecosystems and abundant plant and animal life. This positive concept of wilderness motivates organizations to fight for legislation to preserve such places for biodiversity and recreational enjoyment.

While it is important to protect these types of wilderness areas, it is also important to recognize that viewing nature as a place of escape is evidence of our economic privilege. For much of our planet's human population, "wilderness" is the harsh reality of daily struggle for survival in environmentally degraded places. The term *desertification* refers to the process by which land that was once fertile becomes dry, arid, and unproductive. As humans resort to slash-and-burn agriculture and illegal or mismanaged logging, deserts gradually replace forests, and more human communities struggle to survive in degraded environments. The kinds of wilderness that result from deforestation and desertification are unhealthy, suitable neither as ecological habitats nor as places that sustain human life. Thus, for many of our sisters and brothers around the world, wilderness is more ominous than inspiring.

Impoverished people and poor land are fundamentally connected. Indeed, it is a sad fact that the poorest of human communities often struggle to survive in the worst of environments. Their wilderness areas are characterized by overpopulation, poor soil quality, unsanitary water sources, deforestation—and are extremely vulnerable to natural disasters such as earthquakes, mudslides, drought, and tropical storms. For these communities, the wilderness is not a place to escape to, but something to escape from, and yet it is also their habitat and home.

Our response to the suffering of our fellow human beings is a key component of the final stewardship relationship of Human–Human. In this session, we will examine Christ's ministry of spiritual and physical healing in order to better understand what it means to bring the good news of God's kingdom to the poor and oppressed.

Christ's Ministry of Healing

"Your faith has healed you." (Luke 8:48)

Jesus called his first disciples to leave their livelihoods and "follow me." At the end of his ministry on earth, Jesus gave these disciples authority to "go and make disciples of all nations" (Matthew 28:19). Christians refer to this command as the Great Commission. A disciple is simply one who follows. In identifying ourselves as followers of Christ, Christians seek to model our lives after that of Jesus. Therefore, in order to best respond to Christ's command to "make disciples," we must understand the nature of Christ and his ministry.

In describing the earthly work of Jesus, we can use the word *holism* to refer to the belief that the spiritual and the physical are not separate, but interrelated. Jesus' incarnation demonstrates this holism: Jesus is simultaneously fully spiritual as God and fully physical as human. Christ's ministry was also holistic in that it addressed the whole person, emphasizing both spiritual and physical healing.

In Luke's Gospel account, Jesus begins his ministry by identifying himself as the fulfillment of Isaiah's prophecy: "He has sent me to proclaim freedom for the prisoners and recovery of sight for the blind, to release the oppressed, to proclaim the year of the Lord's favor" (Luke 4:18-19). These tasks become a central theme of Jesus' ministry, which focuses on healing the body as well as the soul, releasing those who believe in him from both physical and spiritual bondage.

Christ offers healing in all areas of life. As disciples of Jesus, we respond to the Great Commission by working to bring this gospel of healing to all people in all nations.

- Read Matthew 4:23-25. What activities are involved in Jesus' ministry?
- Read Mark 2:1-12. What does Jesus tell the paralytic? How does the man experience Christ's holistic healing?
- Read Mark 1:32-34. Who is affected by Christ's healing?

The Least of These

"The poor go about their labor of foraging food." (Job 24:5)

As Jesus taught about God's kingdom and healed people of their physical and spiritual diseases, he also emphasized the importance of caring for the most vulnerable. In Jesus' words, our call as his disciples is to care for "the least of these" (Matthew 25:40). Who are the least of these in our world today? Whom does Christ call us to serve? Just as in Jesus' day, these are the poor and oppressed among our human brothers and sisters. Simply identifying our fellow human beings who are most suffering is not enough, however. In order to offer the healing of Christ to these brothers and sisters, we must understand not just *that* they suffer, but *why* they suffer.

When we identify the least of these, we discover that human suffering is tied to the suffering of creation. If we take seriously Christ's model of proclaiming good news to the poor, we must acknowledge that economic poverty and impoverished land cannot be separated. We who live in economically prosperous nations have the ability to shield ourselves to a great extent from the consequences of environmental degradation, but impoverished communities have no such buffer.

While we can choose where to buy our homes, many are forced to live in crowded slums where disease spreads through unsanitary water sources. While we can shop for our food from the stocked shelves of tidy grocery stores, many are forced to eat whatever they can salvage from the city dump. As our environment continues to suffer from deforestation, pollution, global warming, desertification, and devastating storms, these communities continue to be the least of these, not just because of their economic deprivation, but also because of their poor habitat. Engaging in activities that contribute to environmental healing, then, is part of a proper response to Christ's call to care for those of our brothers and sisters who suffer the most.

- Read Isaiah 61:1-2. In fulfilling this prophecy (see Luke 4:18-19), to whom has Jesus come to preach the good news?
- Read Matthew 25:34-46. How does Jesus describe God in this parable? How does a good steward serve others in a way that honors the king? What physical needs are mentioned?
- Read Job 24:1-12. What images of poverty occur in this passage? How is poverty linked with the environment? What

word is used to describe the wilderness (v. 5)? What is our responsibility to people who suffer because of poor habitat conditions?

Wilderness Restored

"I will turn the desert into pools of water, and the parched ground into springs." (Isaiah 41:18)

In the Old Testament, the wilderness is usually a place of exile and isolation, and those traveling through the wilderness experience hunger and thirst. The biblical notion of wilderness is similar to the reality in which the poor currently struggle to survive. The biblical vision of restored wilderness offers hope for environmentally degraded habitats—places that have become wastelands—in the twenty-first century. Throughout the Bible, restoration of barren wilderness into fertile land parallels the restoration of spiritual relationship with God. Just as all things, including the natural world, suffer as a result of human sin, all things are promised transformation as a result of God's restorative work. The ground of Eden is cursed in Genesis, but the tree of life appears again in Revelation, bearing fruit year round. After wandering in the arid desert for forty years, the Israelites enter the Promised Land, the land "flowing with milk and honey" (Exodus 3:8). Furthermore, God promises to relieve the suffering of the "poor and needy" by causing rivers to flow through dry land and by planting trees in the desert (Isaiah 41:17). We can hope for this healing of habitat because it is part of the Creator's covenant with the work of creation.

Therefore, as Christians, we proclaim the good news of Christ's healing to all of creation—to creation's suffering creatures and to their suffering habitats. Engaging in actions that help to heal the land and reverse ecologically destructive patterns is part of proclaiming the good news of Jesus. The hope that motivates such action is not simply wishful thinking about the future, but the confident expectation that God will fulfill the promises made to creation and to God's people. As the prophet Isaiah joyfully exclaims,

"How beautiful on the mountains are the feet of those who bring good news, who proclaim peace, who bring good tidings, who proclaim salvation" (Isaiah 52:7). Yes, we serve a good God who loves creation and has promised to heal all of its wounds. How lovely indeed are the feet of those who bring this good news of healing to the mountains and to their inhabitants!

- Read Isaiah 41:17-20. What does the healthy land symbolize? How are the needs of people met by their habitats in these visions?
- Read Revelation 22:1-5. What elements of creation are represented here in this final vision of God's reign? What role does creation have in the work of healing?

In Action

1. Identify suffering communities around you. What is contributing to their suffering? Develop a plan for how you can respond to both their physical and spiritual suffering.
2. Participate in a project together that is focused on meeting physical needs: for example, build a house with Habitat for Humanity, or volunteer at a local homeless shelter.
3. Consider becoming a partner with Plant With Purpose and participating in Sponsor a Village or one of our other programs!

Conclusion

Window on the World: Despite the afternoon heat, the small group of women sets out to gather water, but their journey is not the long trek that their mothers and grandmothers used to make. The streambeds closer to their village now flow with clear, clean water. Once-barren mountains and hillsides have been planted again with trees, which begin to grow together into a healthy forest. The women walk beneath its shade and hear the sounds of birds that have returned to their natural habitat. Flooding and mudslides are less widespread. The soil on the forest floor no longer washes away when it rains, and the ground soaks up water to replenish aquifers, rivers, and streams. These women and their communities will continue to depend on the environment for daily survival, but now the land and its people have both begun to experience healing.

Relationships Revisited

In this study, we have examined four relationships that a holistic Christian environmental ethic must address. The first lesson addressed the foundational relationship for any ethic of care for the natural world, the relationship between the Creator and creation. The simplest response to the question, "Why should Christians care about the environment?" is "Because God does." Creation is inherently good, and it reveals and glorifies God. This relationship between the Creator and creation is one of covenant, for God has promised to restore creation to its intended state of shalom.

After recognizing the value of creation in the eyes of God, we turned to examine the relationship between God and human beings, who have a unique role within creation as God's image-bearers. We recovered an understanding of dominion that is modeled on the servant leadership of Jesus and thus approaches creation with humility. Stewardship rooted in humility recognizes that God has given humans dominion over creation in order to serve and to protect it.

Without this properly balanced approach to dominion, creation suffers. In the third lesson, we explored the relationship between humans and their habitats. Because humans are intimately connected with the earth, creation suffers as a result of human sin. God invites humans to participate in the act of restoration by humbling themselves and pursuing healthy spiritual relationship with the Lord.

In the final lesson, we discovered that the relationship between humans and their habitats is one in which poor human communities and impoverished land are fundamentally linked. We considered Christ's ministry as one of both spiritual and physical healing. Providing the model for holistic ministry, Jesus' emphasis on the whole person compels us to address issues of spiritual *and* physical health when reaching out to our neediest brothers and sisters around the world. Because the poor are so connected to their environment, this must include environmental health. Finally, we rejoiced in the hope that the good news of Christ offers to creation's creatures and their habitats—both spiritual and physical restoration.

- What does each of the four relationships of stewardship mean for you and your life?
- What is your hope for restoration in each relationship?

Stewardship Rediscovered

Our understanding of stewardship has been rounded out by exploring these relationships and the ways in which they interact.

What, then, is a good steward? Above all, a good steward acknowledges that creation belongs to God, who loves everything that has been made, calling it "very good." When we see creation through God's eyes, we see that God is revealed in and glorified by this wondrous symphony playing all around us. The good steward knows that humans have a special part to play in this symphony. Made in God's image, humans have a responsibility to care for creation, and thus the good steward seeks to exercise dominion with the same compassion with which God rules. The good steward's attitude is best described as one of humility. With humility, the good steward works to serve and protect creation, acknowledging human dependence on habitat. Because humans are so dependent on habitat, the good steward responds to Christ's call to care for "the least of these" by responding to the ecological degradation that characterizes the habitats of our world's poorest communities.

- How and why are Christians called to take care of creation?
- How has your understanding of stewardship changed?
- How can your church community model stewardship of all of its resources, including natural resources?

Ministry Re-envisioned

Is the revised image of reforested hillsides and clean rivers possible? We must hope that it is not just possible, but that it is promised. If this vision of shalom is, indeed, both possible and promised, then Christians have something very important to say to the larger environmental community. With a proper understanding of stewardship, the Christian voice can offer hope for what often seem like overwhelming problems and futile efforts. Perhaps it is not just possible to be both a Christian and an environmentalist, but also necessary. Christians not only have a voice, but a responsibility: a full understanding of the work of Christ must extend love to our environment and should motivate Christians to work for a healthy planet.

- How would a full understanding of stewardship inform your choices in ministry?
- What can you do as an individual to model an ethic of Christian environmental stewardship? As a family? As a congregation? Create a plan that embodies this ethic.

Take Action—
Make an Impact

As an Individual

- Spend some quiet time outside in God's creation.
- Learn about your local environment. What plants grow there? What creatures thrive there? How is it unique?
- Turn off the faucet when brushing your teeth.
- Turn off the lights when leaving the room.
- Buy secondhand clothes and furniture.
- Bike, walk, or carpool to work or the store.
- Combine errands into one trip.
- Carry a travel mug or water bottle for beverages throughout the day.
- Eat less meat.
- Volunteer to help people less fortunate than you.
- Carry a handkerchief instead of disposable tissues.
- Pray about and consider adopting a simpler lifestyle.

As a Family or Household

- Place an empty mason jar or brick in your toilet tank to save gallons of water every flush.
- When using a dishwasher, turn the heat off and let dishes air dry by opening the door after the cycle has run.
- Air dry clothes instead of using the dryer.
- Wash clothes in cold water.
- Install power strips on electronic items and turn them off completely when not in use.

- Turn the thermostat up three degrees in the summer and down three degrees in the winter.
- Shop at farmer's markets or buy locally grown food.
- Recycle.
- Pre-cycle by considering the packaging waste of items you buy.
- Change the light bulbs in your home to compact fluorescents.
- Use cloth napkins in your home.
- Play outside with your kids more often.
- Clean or replace the air filters in your house.
- Start a family compost pile for green waste.

As a Church Community

- Have a Creation Stewardship Sunday with teachings and activities on creation care.
- Pray for those who are impoverished because of environmental degradation.
- Organize a Trash for Trees fundraiser. (For information, visit www.PlantWithPurpose.org.)
- Start a church recycling project to raise money for ministry.
- Sponsor a village where Plant With Purpose is working to reverse poverty and deforestation.
- Begin a community garden ministry and donate the produce to a soup kitchen.
- Have your church conduct an energy audit to see where it may save money and resources.
- Encourage other groups to use this Bible study to learn about stewardship.
- Host an alternative Christmas fair where shoppers can purchase sustainable items, or donate to good causes in lieu of the Christmas frenzy.
- Begin a tool or toy library in your church to share resources.
- Volunteer for trail building, clean up, or invasive species removal at a local park.
- Organize a team or committee at your church to encourage creation care and commit to it on an ongoing basis.

Creation Care Resources

Further Reading

Abbaté, Michael. *Gardening Eden: How Creation Care Will Change Your Faith, Your Life and Our World*. Colorado Springs, CO: WaterBrook Press, 2009.

Bouma-Prediger, Steven. *For the Beauty of the Earth A Christian Vision for Creation Care (Engaging Culture)*. Grand Rapids: Baker Academic, 2001.

Brown, Edward R. *Our Father's World: Mobilizing the Church to Care for Creation*. Downers Grove, IL: IVP Books, 2006.

DeWitt, Calvin B. *Earth-Wise a Biblical Response to Environmental Issues*. Grand Rapids: CRC Publications, 1994.

Lowe, Ben. *Green Revolution*. Downers Grove, IL: IVP Books, 2009.

Robinson, Tri, and Jason Chatraw. *Saving God's Green Earth: Rediscovering the Church's Responsibility to Environmental Stewardship*. Grand Rapids: Ampelon, 2006.

Robinson, Tri. *Small Footprint, Big Handprint: How to Live Simply and Love Extravagantly*. Boise: Ampelon, 2008.

Sleeth, Matthew, J. *Serve God, Save the Planet: A Christian Call to Action*. Boston: Zondervan Company, 2007.

Sleeth, Nancy, *Go Green, Save Green: A Simple Guide to Saving Time, Money, and God's Green Earth*. Carol Stream, IL: Tyndale House Publishers, 2009.

Creation Care Organizations

A Rocha International (www.arocha.org). An international conservation organization working to care for God's world.

Care of Creation (www.careofcreation.net). Care of Creation is an environmental and missions organization formed in 2005 to bring together two important themes: Love for God's people, and love for God's world.

Creation Care Study Program (www.creationcsp.org) is a high-caliber academic semester abroad connecting Christian faith with the most complex, urgent global issues of the coming decades. CCSP offers programs in Belize and New Zealand.

Evangelical Environmental Network (EEN) and *Creation Care* (www.creationcare.org). A network of individuals and organizations working to "declare the Lordship of Christ over all creation" (Colossians 1:15-20). Magazine is published quarterly.

Flourish (www.flourishonline.org). A collaborative ministry that inspires and equips churches to better love God by reviving human lives and the landscapes on which they depend.

National Religious Partnership for the Environment (NRPE) (www.nrpe.org). An association of independent faith groups undertaking scholarship, leadership training, congregational and agency initiative, and public policy education in service to environmental sustainability and justice.

Plant With Purpose (www.PlantWithPurpose.org). A Christian nonprofit organization working to reverse deforestation and poverty in the world by transforming the lives of the rural poor.

Renewal (www.renewingcreation.org). A Christ-centered creation care network that works with college students and focuses on living in right relationship with God.

Restoring Eden (www.restoringeden.org). A parachurch ministry dedicated to encouraging faithful stewardship of the natural world as a biblical, moral, and wise value.